P9-AQP-009

ANNALS OF
THE NEW YORK ACADEMY
OF SCIENCES

Volume 727

EDITORIAL STAFF

Executive Editor
BILL BOLAND

Managing Editor
JUSTINE CULLINAN

The New York Academy of Sciences
2 East 63rd Street
New York, New York 10021

American Psychological Association
750 First Street, N.E.
Washington, D.C. 20002

ASPECTS OF THE HISTORY OF PSYCHOLOGY IN AMERICA: 1892-1992

ANNALS OF THE NEW YORK ACADEMY OF SCIENCES

Volume 727

ASPECTS OF THE HISTORY OF PSYCHOLOGY IN AMERICA: 1892–1992

Edited by Helmut E. Adler and Robert W. Rieber

The New York Academy of Sciences
New York, New York

American Psychological Association
Washington, D.C.

1994

Cover: The photographs on the cover of the paperbound version of this book are (from left to right) of G. Stanley Hall, James McKeen Cattell, and William James.

Library of Congress Cataloging-in-Publication Data

Aspects of the history of psychology in America : 1892–1992 / edited by Helmut E. Adler and Robert W. Rieber.
    p.   cm. — (Annals of the New York Academy of Sciences ; v. 727)
    Papers presented at a workshop at the Academy on Feb. 15, 1992.
    Includes bibliographical references and index.
    ISBN 0-89766-866-9. — ISBN 0-89766-867-7 (pbk.)
    1. Psychology—United States—History—19th century—Congresses.
2. Psychology—United States—History—20th century—Congresses.
I. Adler, Helmut E.   II. Rieber, R. W. (Robert W.)   III. Series.
BF108.U5A87 1994
150'.973—dc20
                                                            94-42028
                                                            CIP

Printed in the United States of America
ISBN 0-89766-866-9 (cloth)
ISBN 0-89766-867-7 (paper)
ISSN 0077-8923

ANNALS OF THE NEW YORK ACADEMY OF SCIENCES

Volume 727
December 30, 1994

ASPECTS OF THE HISTORY OF PSYCHOLOGY IN AMERICA: 1892–1992[a]

Editors
HELMUT E. ADLER AND ROBERT W. RIEBER

CONTENTS

[a] This volume is the result of a workshop held by the Psychology Section of the New York Academy of Sciences on February 15, 1992 in New York, New York to celebrate the 175th anniversary of the New York Academy of Sciences and the 100th anniversary of the American Psychological Association.

Financial assistance was received from:
  • THE AMERICAN PSYCHOLOGICAL ASSOCIATION
  • PFIZER-ROERIG CORPORATION

Preface

HELMUT E. ADLER

Department of Psychology
Yeshiva University
500 West 185th Street
New York, New York 10033

ROBERT W. RIEBER

Department of Psychology
John Jay College of Criminal Justice
New York, New York 10019

The year 1992 was the centennial year of the founding of the American Psychological Association (APA). It was founded on July 8, 1892 in the study of G. Stanley Hall, Professor of Psychology at Clark University. In addition, 1992 also marked the 175th anniversary of the founding of the Lyceum of Natural History, forerunner of the New York Academy of Sciences. The Lyceum was started on January 29, 1817 by Samuel Latham Mitchill, Professor of Natural History at the College of Physicians and Surgeons. The origins of the APA were closely intertwined with the activities of the Academy a century ago. James McKeen Cattell, Professor of Psychology at Columbia University, was one of the 26 charter members of the APA and was active in promoting a section of Anthropology, Psychology and Philology at the New York Academy of Sciences.

It seemed very appropriate, therefore, for the current Section of Psychology to call for a scientific meeting to commemorate these milestones. We arranged such a meeting, with speakers selected from active researchers in the history of psychology. The meeting was held as a workshop at the Academy on February 15, 1992, with the title *Aspects of the History of Psychology in America, 1892–1992: In celebration of The New York Academy of Sciences' 175th Anniversary and the American Psychological Association's 100th Anniversary.* The meeting was supported in part by contributions from the American Psychological Association and from Pfizer-Roerig Corporation. Their contributions are gratefully acknowledged. We are also grateful to Charles Wiener, whose photographs of the participants at the workshop are shown on pages x and xi.

The conference opened with greetings from the Academy by Section Chair Ellen M. Richter and from the American Psychological Association by Chief Science Officer Frances Degen Horowitz. The opening address was presented by Seymour B. Sarason, who was introduced by Paul Wachtel. Sarason stressed the lack of historical knowledge on the part of today's students. In his chapter "A Personal View of the History of American

Psychology," he pointed out that history deserves more emphasis since today's students are ignorant of even the most important historical events. He goes on to mention that not only does American psychology lack a historiography worthy of the name, but even the history that *is* taught neglects the indigenous element of our own history.

In his contribution "James McKeen Cattell, the New York Academy of Sciences, and the American Psychological Association 1891–1902," Michael Sokal illuminates how one man, namely Cattell, played a leading role in the growth of both organizations. Few have done so much for institutional science as James McKeen Cattell. In what qualifies as a historian's chapter, Sokal bases his commentary on primary sources.

Next, Eugene Taylor discusses the sometimes stormy relationship of G. Stanley Hall and William James. In considering G. Stanley Hall's motives for waiting until William James was out of town to found the APA, Taylor traces the differences in personality and intellectual approach between the two men.

In a paper that he originally delivered in his capacity of historian for the Eastern Psychological Association (EPA), Ludy T. Benjamin, Jr. focuses on the origins of that body, offering a history of the New York Branch of the American Psychological Association.

Joseph Jastrow founded a psychological laboratory in distant Wisconsin and was an early writer of popular psychology. "Joseph Jastrow: Pioneer Psychologist Facing the 'Administrative Peril,'" is the title of chapter by Arthur Blumenthal, who writes of the conflict between faculty and the growing power of the administration in university life. Jastrow opposed, together with others, the dictatorial style of presidency then coming into vogue.

The next contributor to this volume is Laurel Furumoto, whose chapter "Christine Ladd-Franklin's Color Theory: Strategy for Claiming Scientific Authority" traces the trials and tribulations of Ladd-Franklin's attempts to have her theory of color vision accepted by the scientific establishment. Furumoto views this struggle within the wider framework of Ladd-Franklin's attempt to claim scientific authority. This struggle was especially important to her as a woman in an era that gave little encouragement to women's scientific careers.

Women's contributions to psychology also were the focus of Elizabeth Scarborough's chapter, "Recognition for Women: The Problem of Linkage." Although women were active participants in meetings and in government during the first 30 years of the APA, the next 50 years represent a period during which women were not given status or recognized in proportion to their numbers. Only in the last 20 years has there been a move to equalize recognition. The source of the discrepancy has been a lack of linkage between accomplishment and recognition.

Looking at the changes that have taken place in the profession, Helmut E. Adler compares the value of a German Ph.D. in 1892 with that in 1942 in his chapter "The European Influence on American Psychology: 1892 and 1942." Wherereas a German degree or even study abroad enhanced one's job chances in 1892, in 1942 it was a handicap, since the field was crowded with the many distinguished European emigrés coming into the United States at that time

Donald K. Freedheim reviews the field of psychotherapy in his chapter "Historical Perspectives on Psychotherapy." He covers its theory, research, practice and training, and concludes with a view toward the future. He takes up not only the problem of psychotherapy itself, but also the economic pressures emerging with respect to third-party payers.

In the following chapter, "Stanley Hall and Company: Observations on the First 100 APA Presidents," John D. Hogan brings out some curious and enlightening facts about the first 100 presidents of the APA. He answers such questions as: which university produced the most presidents and whom to pick as your mentor if you want to be president of the APA. The reader will learn which president was born in Fatehgarh, India, and who was born in Caiazzo, Italy, among those born outside the United States.

Kurt Salzinger tackled the onerous role of discussant in the original meeting on which this collection of papers is based. His contribution "Sitz-fleisch 2: The Platzgeist and Cognitive Environmental Psychology" is a humorous piece, but it also has a satirical bite to it.

In addition to the speakers mentioned above, Robert W. Rieber and Barbara Ross contributed papers. Unfortunately they were not able to include their contributions in the present volume. Ludy Benjamin, Jr., Donald Freedheim, and John Hogan were not present at the workshop, although they were asked to contribute a chapter by the editors. Howard Gruber acted as discussant and Paul Wachtel introduced Seymour Sarason.

The two institutions that we honor in this publication, the American Psychological Association and the New York Academy of Sciences, have grown and prospered in the 100 and 175 years, respectively, since their founding. They have weathered crises and remained vital and active. May they continue to contribute to the growth of science in general and psychology in particular!

ek

The editors acknowledge with thanks the efforts of Mr. Bill Boland of the New York Academy of Sciences and Dr. Gary VandenBos of the American Psychological Association for their efforts to bring about the first joint publication of the two institutions. We would also like to thank Mrs. Justine Cullinan for her editorial work. Finally, we wish to thank our families for their patience and support during the preparation and editing of this volume.

Pictures from the Workshop

Participants at the workshop on the history of psychology in America, held at the New York Academy of Sciences on February 15, 1992. From left to right: Robert Rieber, Elizabeth Scarborough, Helmut Adler, Kurt Salzinger, Barbara Ross, Arthur Blumenthal, Michael Sokal, Laurel Furumoto, Eugene Tayor, and Howard Gruber.

Seymour Sarason, Robert Rieber, Paul Wachtel

Helmut Adler

Arthur Blumenthal

Laurel Furumoto

Howard Gruber

Frances Horowitz

Ellen Richter

Barbara Ross

Seymour Sarason

Kurt Salzinger

Elizabeth Scarborough

Michael Sokal

Eugene Taylor

Foreword

HOWARD E. GRUBER

Department of Developmental and Educational Psychology
Teachers College
Columbia University
New York, New York 10027

The central themes of this volume, sometimes unacknowledged, are growth and struggle. Sometimes struggle is the catalyst for growth, sometimes the midwife. And some struggles have no such saving graces, except to reveal, to those who want the lesson, the ordinariness of eminent academic people.

There were 31 charter members of the American Psychological Association at the time of its formation in 1892; there were about 75,000 members in 1992. In other words, the number has doubled every 10 years. The authors of the present volume deal less with the causes of this growth than with its consequences. But their emphasis is not on the consequent growth of psychological knowledge. Rather, in reading these essays one sees primarily the appearance and working of rivalries, cronyism, bureaucracy, sexism and other forms of discrimination: in short, academic power politics.

These processes, internal to the academic and scientific world, take place in and sometimes directly reflect the character of the larger society that shapes the participants, in particular the emphasis on perpetual competition and growth, and the chronic tendency to exclude some people from the status of full humanity. Still, universities and similar institutions are, to some extent, walled off as havens from the outer world. So it is possible to write a valid part of intellectual history without focussing on the larger context. (But don't worry: some of the relationships between these levels will appear, willy nilly.)

At first, as I read the manuscript and began to get the picture, it offended me. For I too, like the psychologists depicted here, have lived my adult life inside the field, and have devoted a large fund of energy to research, teaching, and various efforts for social betterment, and, as I believe, with only modest and occasional participation in the stupefying and self-aggrandizing rituals of institutional combat.

But as I read on, first I was pulled into the drama of this collective historical enterprise emphasizing all sorts of conflict. Then I began to see that there is a worthwhile intellectual task here: to understand the working out of the themes of institutional growth and struggle as they unfold in the setting of institutions and individuals that have as their stated mission education and intellectual work. Finally, this collection of papers brought me to realize that such institutional patterns are the societal context within which intellectual work goes on, and, I hope, sometimes goes forward.

To some extent these juggernauts create the human frailties that trouble me, and to some extent they merely exploit them. For better or worse, and with all their faults, these institutions have come to be the societal instruments that foster intellectual work, even though they often stunt or distort it. My sense of proportion (or of resignation?) by these thoughts restored, I feel readier now to discuss some of the issues raised in the present volume.

The exclusion of women from full participation in the academic life, even the most accomplished women, although by now a familiar story, still comes as a shock when we encounter a new example. Furumoto tells Christine Ladd-Franklin's story well and draws a surprising conclusion, that Ladd-Franklin's primary motive in publishing a book of her papers was to gain recognition from the male academic community. While I gladly concede the right of women to chase after fame as much as men do, it seems to me that a productive scientist may have more than one motive for her or his efforts, including the more "intrinsic" motive of bringing one's work to people's attention because she or he believes it to be important.

Among the varieties of conflictual experience, Sarason's paper is perhaps the most filled with yearning: the wish to understand and to be understood, to understand American psychology and culture; the wish to be understood as a Jew, as an American, as a prewar psychologist; the hope that through these understandings will come a better grasp of world psychology, and ultimately psychology's fulfilment of its potential for contributing to world peace. With yearning comes the possibility of frustration, and for Sarason one of the forms it takes is his dismay at the ignorance of the past displayed by his students. Who was John Dewey? Have you read anything by William James? Putting such questions to students does not lead to very satisfying answers.

In what sense, then, does Sarason's essay express struggle? I believe he wants to struggle against the ravages of time, the decay of historical identity as part of his students' (and his discipline's) heritage. How does this historical decay connect with the issue of growth? Through the restless movement of intellectual fashions in psychology, history is squeezed out. He writes: "Indeed, just as these students had never read Barker, Dewey, Brown, Dollard, and De Tocqueville, they had never been exposed to the concept of reductionism, with its temptations, its dangers, as well as its valid uses in the history of psychology" (p. x). But he is not proposing the study of history as a scholarly enterprise. His underlying concern is for each student to develop a sense of personal identity. Among his other proposals is the idea that each graduate student should be encouraged to write his or her autobiography, not as a private confessional, but as a search for intellectual identity. And this is an inner form of struggle.

Other forms of struggle are detailed in these essays. I can only touch on a few examples.

The individual against the institution: Jastrow relates how the young Harry Israel was required to change his name to Harry Harlow before he could be appointed to the faculty of the University of Wisconsin. Blumenthal's essay is appropriately titled "Joseph Jastrow: Pioneer Pyschologist Facing the 'Administrative Peril.'" Jastrow's professional life witnessed the growth of the University President as a recognized and potent concentration of power, depriving the faculties of control of their institutions. Not surprisingly, there was an organized movement against this development, And not surprisingly, it failed. The universities were competing for a distinguished faculty, for higher student enrollments, for more buildings. A president who could play the corporate game was more valuable than a professor-turned-president who could only be an intellectual leader.

And it must be said, too, that the theme of prolonged rivalry between intellectual combatants is not a minor feature of the academic arena. Intellectual and institutional rivalries merge in the accounts by Sokal (on Cattell), by Taylor (on James and Hall), and by Benjamin (on the New York Branch of the APA). Rivalries between Harvard, Clark, Johns Hopkins, and Columbia universities are depicted and proprietary questions are sorted out: Who established the first psychological laboratory? Who pioneered the importation of psychoanalysis to the United States?

When I was an undergraduate (1939–1943), the principal theories contending for our allegiance were *Gestalttheorie,* behaviorism, and psychoanalysis (or one of its modernizations, such as Horney's work, which made room for cultural and societal factors). Piaget was not "rediscovered" in America until the 1950s, or even later. Tolman's cognitive behaviorism, quite friendly to Gestalt psychology, was part of the scene. (I remember writing a paper, "Rats can think!" in a Tolmanian vein.)

Even though the predominant mode of discussion was the confrontation between theories, this could be done in different styles. Michael Wertheimer and D. Brett King (1994) have recently described the stylistic differences between Köhler and Max Wertheimer. Köhler was tense and disputatious; Wertheimer was friendly and respectful. After a meeting between Wertheimer and Hull, in which the former commented on a draft of the latter's APA presidential address, Hull wrote a friendly note: "As so often happens, the persons who do not entirely agree with us are the very ones who really help us the most." A common phrase one encountered in informal arguments was "That can be translated," meaning that what you are saying in your theoretical language can be said, and better, in mine. Not a cataclysmic outcome, but a theoretical confrontation, none the less.

Helmut Adler's essay on the European influence provides a valuable picture of the influx of European psychologists into American academic life, giving considerable attention to the Gestalt psychologists leaving Nazi Germany. By stopping at the year 1942, Adler simplified his task in a useful way, but he omitted the importation of developmental thinking under the banners of Piaget and, more recently, Vygotsky. Especially in the period shaped by the Nazi menace, the role of psychologists in rescuing their colleagues has been vital. Among the Gestaltists, Wertheimer was active in this work. In her essay, "One Man against the Nazis," in a different volume, Mary Henle (1986) has given a stirring account of Köhler's struggles to save the Berlin Psychological Institute until he was forced to retire, then migrating to the United States and a post at Swarthmore College.

None of the transplanted Gestalt psychologists received full appointments at Harvard or other similarly prestigious schools. But in fairness it should be said that Wertheimer was offered a post at Harvard and refused it in favor of the New School for Social Research, which, for its exceptional role in accommodating refugee scholars, became known as the University in Exile—and more informally, when I was there, "the Weimar Republic."

Several of the papers in this volume deal with seemingly strictly organizational questions, such as the emergence of regional associations to solve problems of travel in our large country. But lightly concealed in such geographical issues were divisive ideological ones, such as the appropriate emphases to be put on research versus applied psychology. The formation of the Eastern Psychological Association set the tone for a long-standing separation of these interests. A similar split has led to the recent formation of the American Psychological Society.

A large and expanding profession in an enormous country leaves room for the emergence of new groups to express new concerns. Not all of the emergent groups are expressions of narrow professional interests. Among the new divisions of the APA recently formed are several dealing with specialized approaches to social issues: population and environment, family psychology, lesbian and gay concerns, and ethnic minority concerns. The most recent of these is the vigorous and promising Division of Peace Psychology. It is noteworthy that this kind of organizational growth does not proceed top-down from wise people at the top to quiescent and acquiescent members at the bottom. Far more typically, an *ad hoc* committee is first formed, often around a very specific issue. This leads to an unaffiliated organization, which proposes the creation of a new division within the APA. Back at the beginning of this process there may have been only a handful of individuals who saw the need and put the necessary vision and energy into the pipeline.

To return to Christine Ladd-Franklin for a moment: all her life she struggled for the recognition she deserved for her theory of color vision. Ironically, hers was an irenic theory, expressing a quest for synthesis by showing how the Young–Helmholtz theory could be reconciled with the

Hering theory, since one referred to the level of sensory mechanisms and the other to the level of perceptual experience. But the prevailing style (masculine?) of discussion was confrontation and choice, rather than integration. So, not only was a woman excluded from her proper place in the scientific arena, but also an opportunity for integrative thought was missed.

In a recent paper Gibson (1994) has analyzed 95 published presidential addresses to the APA. He concludes from this and other studies that "in the future, psychology, as a whole, will continue to grow even more diverse, specialized, utilitarian, and professional-organizational." To my mind, that is the bad news. The good news is that there will remain a large number of psychologists striving to make psychology more integrative, more humane, and more socially responsible.

REFERENCES

GIBSON, K. R. 1994. The Presidential Addresses of the American Psychological Association, 1892–1992: A qualitative analysis. Hist. Psychol. Newslett. 26: 16–24.

HENLE, M. 1986. One man against the Nazis. In 1879 and All That: Essays in the Theory and History of Psychology. M. Henle, Ed.: 225–237. Columbia University Press. New York.

WERTHEIMER, M. & D. B. KING. 1994. Max Wertheimer's American sojourn, 1933–1943. Hist. Psychol. Newslett. 26: 3–15.

A Personal View of the History of American Psychology

SEYMOUR B. SARASON

Yale University
2 Hillhouse Avenue
New Haven, Connecticut 06520

In the course of our lives we experience the anniversary of our birth in changing ways. For as a very young child, the observance of this date is not an occasion for personal review, nor does it prompt one to try to glimpse the future. But slowly and subtly with the passage of years, our birth date becomes an occasion when, whether we like it or not, the past and future are no longer, so to speak, "independent variables," but become more and more closely connected arenas of thought. So, as Samuel Johnson said, nothing concentrates the mind so powerfully as the knowledge that you will die tomorrow. A poet once said that life takes its final meaning in chosen death, by which he meant, I assume, that such a choice is an expression of judgment both about choices made in the past and the one which will govern the future.

The developmental history of the experience of anniversaries has not caught the interest of psychologists, a fact of which I was unaware until I found myself intrigued with the daunting thought that I wanted to write my professional autobiography. That I knew my years were numbered goes without saying, but that knowledge hardly justified the writing of an autobiography, which would inevitably have to be personal and professional. Nor could I justify my wish as an indulgence of *chutzpah,* an attribute I know I did not lack. I also knew that the professional world of psychology neither needed nor desired my autobiography. But *chutzpah* and reality testing need not be uncorrelated. So, granted that personal decisions are multiply determined, on what reasonable grounds could I justify writing the autobiography? Those grounds began to become clear when I told a colleague what I was planning, ending with the statement, "Psychology needs my autobiography like it needs a hole in the head." And when I said that I realized that I had long felt that American psychology had more than one hole in its head. But now I knew it with a conviction derived from the knowledge that my days were numbered. So what? Why not write another article or a sequel to my book *Psychology Misdirected* (1981)? Long being a theatergoer, I knew that playwrights tend to run downhill after the first act, a fact that in no way means that the first act was all that good. And how many sequels to successful movies have passed muster?

1

The fog of indecision began to dissipate in the light of two considerations, which were in the nature of insights. The first was that if my critiques of American psychology had any validity I should be able to demonstrate it in my personal-professional history, by going beyond (or beneath) discussion of theory and research, or the merits of this or that trend or point of view. For example, I have written a fair amount about psychology's inability, unwillingness, or blindness vis-à-vis the need to address any conception of the *social* in other than dyadic or small-group contexts. How many times have I said that American psychology is an asocial, individual psychology from which you get the most narrow, distorted conception of the American society whose citizens that psychology purports to understand? How many times must I plead that psychology should take seriously such works as J. F. Brown's *Psychology and the Social Order* (1936), John Dollard's *Criteria for the Life History* (1935), and De Tocqueville's *Democracy in America*, written in the early nineteenth century? The answer to the last question was clear. Shortly before I began to write my autobiography *The Making of an American Psychologist* (1988), the *American Psychologist* rejected one of my favorite papers, "The Lack of an Overarching Conception in American Psychology" (1989). In that paper I discuss in detail Dollard's scathing and unanswered criticisms of social psychology's tendency to trivial pursuit, this from a man who was originally a sociologist, and then became a psychoanalyst, an anthropologist, and finally a psychologist. Dollard's *Criteria for the Life History* and his *Caste and Class in a Southern Town* (1937) I consider as classics, but in American psychology they have the status of nonbooks.

A larger portion of that paper concerned De Tocqueville. On what conceptual basis, by reference to what system or intuitive grasp of psychology, was this young Frenchman able to portray the psychology of Americans so tellingly that when we read him a hundred fifty years later we can see ourselves? And he was in this country for only nine months! I tried to spell out the ingredients of his implicit psychology and, needless to say, American psychology does not come up smelling like a rose. The editor of the *American Psychologist* and three of its reviewers saw no merit in what I had written. I put the paper in my file-but-do-not-forget drawer. When, several years later, the editor of *Mind and Behavior,* on whose editorial board I serve, asked if I might contribute a paper for the journal, I sent him that very paper. He decided, on his own judgment, to accept it. To me, at least, and for obvious reasons, it is reassuring to reflect that there exists at least one journal editor secure enough to make an independent decision. But I have already said that I do not lack *chutzpah.*

For my present purposes, the quality of that paper is irrelevant. I presented the anecdote in order to make the point that the rejection of the paper encouraged me to cease writing articles, for a while at least, and to use my autobiography to illustrate how I, as person and psychologist, was not understandable according to the regnant conceptions of American psychology. This, I should hasten to add, does not mean that I view American psychology as altogether and irredeemably bankrupt. Let us remember that, for the most part, when you go into bankruptcy, you still have assets. You just do not have enough assets to accomplish your purposes. It is on this analogy that I regard contemporary American psychology, as, in essence, did Brown and Dollard in their own time, and as more than a few others in the present day do also. But there is no bankruptcy law or court which may judge among the liabilities of academic disciplines. Unlike generals, they do not die or fade away, despite the likes of me as creditors.

When I decided in 1988 to write my autobiography, it was infinitely easier than the task that lay before me: to decide how to organize my past so as to demonstrate that neither as person or psychologist was I understandable except in terms of American history. My life was of one piece with a particular time in that history. I was a first-generation Jew, I experienced the rites of passage into a profession, I learned that the concept of luck has no role in conventional theory, I was passionately partisan to a political ideology and to a certain psychological theory, and I was to undergo the wrenching process of unlearning both ideology and theory. Could I make a compelling case that current psychological theories of the personality and social type either singly or collectively could never explain me, that it would be only how I explained myself that would make adequate sense to a reader?

Again I have to say that the merits of my autobiography are irrelevant to my present purposes. What is relevant is that once I decided to write it, I had a second insight: during the last ten years as an active member of my department I had not allowed myself to face up to my disappointment and even anger at what seemed to be an unbridgeable gulf between me and graduate students. Put in another way, students not only had little or no sense of the history of the field, they were not even very interested. To them I went to graduate school somewhat after the battle of Gettysburg. (I retired in 1989).

In one of my seminars I asked some first-year students: How many of you have heard of John Dewey? One student had heard of Dewey, but it turned out that he had taken a philosophy course and had no idea that Dewey had been a psychologist at all, let alone president of the APA in 1899. When I suggested that he read Dewey's 1896 paper on the concept of the reflex arc in psychology if he wanted to understand modern psychology, I received the distinct impression that he thought I ought to take early retirement. This incident put me in mind of an occasion in 1987, when for reasons I cannot now recall, I asked a class what of William James they had read? Four or five had heard of William James. None had read anything by him.

Yale graduate students are as a group bright, eager, likeable, ambitious, sharp characters. But whatever their virtues may be when they come to Yale, a sense of historical identity is not one of them. Of course they expect that by the time they finish their graduate education they will have earned an identity as psychologists. But that identity will be rooted in a near past and a near future. That is not because there is a universal law that says that young people are incapable of a sense of identity based on a much longer perspective on the past or that they have a built-in resistance to acceptance of a continuity with a distant past. In these days when psychologists, psychiatrists, and the mass media regale us with biological-genetic explanations of psychological characteristics—from altruism to shyness to alcoholism and much more—I await an article discussing the biological basis for ignoring or rejecting the past. When I would make remarks such as these to my graduate students, they would listen respectfully but quite skeptically, unaware as they were of the history of reductionism in psychology. Indeed, just as these students had never read Barker, Dewey, Brown, Dollard, and De Tocqueville, they had never been exposed to the concept of reductionism, with its temptations, its dangers, as well as its valid uses in the history of psychology. Nor was their skepticism dented by my saying, "I also came into psychology when biological explanations were frequent. Then the pendulum swung to very complicated psychological explanations. And today we are back to the biological, secure in the feeling that we will not repeat the mistakes of the past, that the swings of the pendulum are due only to new findings of scientific research and are independent of what is happening in the social world. Or could it be that these swings are themselves a reflection of human biology?"

I can assure you that I was not blaming the students who, I made clear, were victims of an undergraduate preparation which was ahistorical in the extreme. And, to make matters worse, it was likely that their graduate education would not repair the damage. Graduate education in psychology does not rest on what I would call a "classical sense," a search for and an acknowledgment of the threads of continuity with our antecedents of the near and distant past. The past is a past we have overcome, not a past any features of which survive usefully into the present.

It used to be that no one could get a doctorate in psychology without having taken a course, or being examined, on the history of psychology. That requirement was no token gesture to icons of the past. It was a requirement by three or four generations of senior psychologists who lived through the divorce of psychology from philosophy and the remarriage of psychology to science. The history was a quest for understanding, justification, and identity. By the time World War II started, the motives for such a quest had noticeably weakened. My exposure to history during my graduate years 1939–1942 at Clark University left me with three clear conclusions and one inchoate question. The three conclusions were: the history of psychology was the history of *ideas*, it was also a history of *individuals*, and it was a history in which psychology differed remarkably from one country to another. The inchoate question was: how do we account for the differences among countries? At the time I did not pose the question quite so clearly. It was more a feeling that something was missing, that there was more to the story than memorizing the ideas and roles of Wundt, Stumpf, Külpe, Ebbinghaus, Bartlett, Hume, Berkeley and others in the pantheon of greats. And nothing in what I was taught explained why Periclean Athens gave rise to individuals with whom some of us still deal in psychology. What we were given was a history of a psychology oriented to the individual and devoid of a social context. There was one exception which stuck in my mind. Somewhere in William James I read something like this: given their jaw-breaking language and their devotion to detail, order, and system, only German psychologists could devise the mind-numbing experiments they did. Being Jewish in those days of Hitler does not wholly explain why I cottoned to James' observation. In an intuitive but inchoate way I recognized that James was putting his finger on an important problem in psychology.

The history to which I was exposed conveyed a subliminal message as potent as it was unverbalized: granted that American psychology had roots in the "Old World," American psychology was nonetheless developing a distinctive and superior psychology, one that gave much greater promise for exposing and illuminating the workings of the human psyche. The obvious did not have to be put into words. It could not have occurred to me explicitly that the message said something, indeed spoke volumes, about Americans and America. I am in no way suggesting that the message was devoid of merit, although that is an arguable point. What I am saying is that the message totally ignored the principle that whatever we mean by human behavior is inexplicable in any comprehensive way apart from contexts within contexts, ranging from the local to the national to the international. The one person, as I said earlier, who clearly posed and studied the problem was the young Frenchman who early in the nineteenth century spent nine months in young America and then wrote a book that continues to startle us with its undiminished power to teach us about the *American individual in American society*. I am aware of no history of American psychology, no history of social psychological theory, that asks the question: What was the "psychology" this man employed that enabled him to reveal us to ourselves? When I am asked what I mean by "contexts within contexts," I refer the questioner to his book. Political science regards that book as one of its classics. Unfortunately, it is a book has no status in asocial, ahistorical American psychology.

That the book has no such status is cause for regret; that the central problems it deals with have little status in mainstream psychology I regard as inexcusable, especially in light of the ways World War II transformed the world and America's place in it. Put it another way, World War II and its aftermath plunged the United States into a role in which it had to deal with peoples and societies truly alien to it. How well were we prepared to confront inevitable yet predictable problems in understanding foreign peoples and their societies? How well did we understand *our own* psychology and the way in which it might help or hinder us in our new role? What did the *discipline* of psychology have to contribute to how we should think and act? The last question in no way assumes that the field of psychology was or could be in a position to influence our foreign relations. But it does assume that, no less than with other fields of inquiry and knowledge (and I would argue more), the transformed world would have an impact on the questions *psychologists as psychologists* would ask or become interested in. How would a psychology that riveted on the individual be affected by what was truly a new world? As citizens, all psychologists cannot have failed to experience, to varying degrees, some shift of world view. It was inevitable that those changes color their view of the role and direction of their field. How, if at all, would psychology change in regard to how it conceived of the relationships between the individual and his society? The change has been the opposite of dramatic.

You would be wrong if, on the basis of what I have said in this centennial year of the American Psychological Association, you predicted that I would call for a greater emphasis in graduate education in the history of psychology. Such an emphasis, I have no doubt, would take the form of courses which would have the counterproductive effect of proving to students that history is about isolated ideas, problems, individuals, and, of course, dates. Anyone familiar with what I have written about curriculum reform in our public schools will know why those efforts end up confirming that the more things change the more they remain the same. So, for example, the curriculum reforms of the turbulent sixties—the new math, the new physics, the new biology, the new social studies—turned out, as I predicted, to be disasters. The effects were not harmless, they were iatrogenic calamities.

All that I have thus far said entered into my decision to write my autobiography as a way of saying to students: "Here is what I think you have to take into account if you want to explain me as person and psychologist. Psychoanalytic theory is indeed relevant, but it is far from sufficient to such a task, and the same is true for those personality, social, developmental, and cognitive theorists who have earned deserved status in the field. In telling my story I aimed to see things whole, knowing full well that I would fall far short of that idea. Of one thing I can assure you, if and when *you* finish *your* story, you will have put flesh on the bones of the abstraction that you contain and your story will reflect a near and far distant past as yet unacknowledged in our theories. Our genes go back a long way. That we know. The stuff of our minds, of our psyches, also goes back a long way. The ways in which we are socialized into our field have not been productive of valid understanding in this regard. All of us know that we are "American" psychologists. But when we use that adjective to describe ourselves, we are using it in its narrow, geographical sense, not in the sense that we are products of a distinctive national history that has put its stamp on us and our field, a history containing a world view that we are not schooled either to examine or articulate, and that in the perverse ways of the dialectic is both freeing and imprisoning."

Somewhere in my autobiography I found myself suggesting that anyone entering graduate school in psychology should be encouraged to write his or her autobiography. I made that suggestion almost as an aside, but the more I have pondered it, the more I have grown to like it, not an unusual fate for our pet ideas. I am reminded here of those early days after World War II when modern clinical psychology was, so to speak, born. Those were also the days when psychoanalysis became legitimated in the university, not only in psychiatry and psychology, but in the other social sciences and in the humanities as well. There were some in psychology who took seriously Freud's dictum that if you were going to accept the responsibility to help others with their personal problems, you should experience the role of patient, submitting yourself and your problems to the scrutiny of an experienced analyst. It is to Freud's everlasting credit that he insisted that there were not two theories: one for patients and another for therapists. There was one theory and anyone who wanted to be an analyst had the moral and professional responsibility to understand that theory in the most personal of ways. So it was not surprising that some psychologists recommended that prospective clinical psychologists should undergo some form and degree of psychotherapy. There were some who recommended that therapy be made a requirement, a strange view of productive learning. Although I was opposed to such a mandate, I accepted the principle that the experience of being a patient could be helpful in one's role as therapist.

I learned a great deal about myself in the course of being psychoanalyzed. But as the years went on, I became increasingly aware that what I had been and what I still was, both as person and psychologist, was by no means explainable by what I had learned in the analysis. It could be argued that psychoanalytic theory is not intended to be an encompassing explanatory framework of human development and behavior, valid regardless of where the development occurred and the behavior patterns which it shaped. And it could be argued that Freud was quite aware that psychoanalytic theory was not sociology, political science, or any other conventional discipline, but rather a set of principles and processes which undergirded those disciplines. Absent that undergirding, these disciplines will remain superficial and fruitless.

There are some who would argue both points today, but to do so would be to read the present into the past. In those earlier days, psychoanalytic theory *was* presented as encompassing and, therefore, in a "successful" analysis, the patient knew why and how he had become the person he was. The possibility that the origins, substance, and development of psychoanalysis were themselves unexplainable by the theory—that religion, ethnicity, national history, and national politics, for example, were parts of an explanation—could not be considered by partisans of the theory.

For example, why did Freud dislike America and, I think, Americans? That question intrigued and bothered me. It reminded me of a letter Freud wrote to Saul Rosenzweig, who was my dissertation advisor at Clark University. Rosenzweig had written to Freud about his experimental studies of repression. The response was a relatively brief letter in which Freud expressed something akin to disdain for Rosenzweig's misdirected efforts. It was not a cordial letter. If the history of psychology I learned at Clark never explained national differences, that letter hanging in Rosenzweig's office was further evidence that national origins represented a very important variable. How important it was became compellingly clear when in my first position after leaving Clark I developed a friendship with Henry Schaefer-Simmern, a political refugee who was an artist, art historian, art theorist, and art educator. I wrote about him in my autobiography and in my recent book *The Challenge of Art to Psychology* (1990). The chasm between his European and my American mind was indeed wide. Whatever psychoanalytic theory could demonstrate about our kinship as humans was more than offset by the differences in our world view. It was Schaefer who subtly and indirectly forced me to confront the fact that I was not just *a* psychologist, but an *American* psychologist.

Let us return to my suggestion that graduate students be encouraged to write their autobiographies. And let us impose the restriction that the student not be asked to write a personal confessional, that is, a hell-diving expedition into the unconscious. What we would be after would be those personal variables, typically favored concepts, or specific characteristics purported to play a role in shaping American lives, and not necessarily only from the point of view of national identity. For example, to belabor the obvious, it is a difference that makes a difference whether the student is male or female. On one occasion I discussed this task with several graduate students, requesting only that they list what they regarded as crucial variables. Of the four males students none listed gender as fateful for their lives. The two female students did list it. When I pressed the male students to explain the omission, they had difficulty doing so. When I further pressed them to explain why the two female students listed gender, it took them a couple of minutes to explain it in terms of how the women's liberation movement had made gender so salient for females. The female students agreed with them.

I then asked this question: "Assuming that as men and women you are representative of graduate students in general, would you expect to observe similar differences in this kind of list in the case of men and women of your age who are not graduate students?" Although they almost immediately said no, they had difficulty explaining their answer. It took a rather long and somewhat torturous discussion for them to implicate social class, religious affiliation, ethnicity, rural-urban differences, and political ideology as variables. Although I did not pursue the inquiry, I am secure in two conclusions. The first is that if I had asked them to list the factors that shaped their personalities, they would not have hesitated to mention parents, family relationships, schooling, and certain particular individuals, for instance, a teacher or a friend. The second is that they would have not have mentioned that they were Americans. They see themselves as unique individuals explainable by intrapsychic, interpersonal, individual-developmental variables. They are in no doubt that in a most narrow and restricted sense their private psychological world has a strictly psychological history, one that they are more or less competent to examine. What they almost totally lack is an awareness of what the gestaltists emphasized: a figure always has a ground, and we ignore the ground until conditions cause us to reverse figure and ground. In that sense, every personality theory I know about either ignores the figure-ground complementarity or pays only lip service to its existence.

When I was a graduate student in 1939–1942, I knew no one who had been outside the country. That changed dramatically after World War II. In recent decades I asked students who had been abroad to identify what, if anything, surprised them in their travels? Their answers fell into three categories. The first can be put this way: "I was not prepared for how *old* everything looked. For the first time I knew what was meant by the New and Old worlds." The second category can be put this way: "In France you saw only Frenchmen and you could eat only French food. The same in Italy. I never realized how heterogeneous the United States was in terms of people and food." The third category is summed up in the first sentence of a tour book on Italy I read before my first trip abroad: "Remember, every Italian is two thousand years old." Categories aside, what I found so interesting about the reactions of the students (as well as of my own) was that they knew in some rudimentary way that if they wanted to comprehend the "psychology" of Frenchmen or Italians they had to take account of factors not contained in our American theories of human behavior. That, of course, is what they would have to do if they wanted to comprehend themselves as Americans.

For a few years after World War II there were major points of intersection between American psychology and anthropology. The study of culture and personality took on a significance that gave promise to achieving an overarching conception of human behavior. It was not fortuitous that Harvard's short-lived Department of Social Relations was formed then to include psychologists, anthropologists, and sociologists. A similar, more ambitious predecessor was Yale's Institute of Human Relations, which flourished in the thirties and forties. It housed the departments of psychology, psychiatry, and part of anthropology. Edward Sapir was brought there from the University of Chicago, and he brought John Dollard with him. No one more than Sapir pursued the goal of integrating the social sciences. By the fifties it was clear that that pursuit was losing steam as each field retreated to parochial concerns. That retreat is not explainable, except in small measure, to personality and organizational factors. It was a retreat, a renewed schism, between two very different conceptions of the primary mission of the social sciences. Psychology has never felt at home with conceptions that went far beyond the individual organism.

Centennials are occasions for celebrations. Voltaire said that history is written by the victors. And it is the victors that our graduate students read. Psychology does have cause for celebration and it is well that our students know that. But, and there always is a *but,* what our students need to know is that precisely because it is an *American* celebration there is a built-in source of error and distortion in what the victors write. If there is anything we do well in graduate education, it is to sensitize students to the crucial importance of eliminating personal bias in conducting research. But, again the *but,* we do an extraordinarily poor job of sensitizing students to the possibility that our theories of human behavior have a distinctively American bias which, far from seeking to minimize, we should seek to uncover, if only to understand ourselves better. Psychology's theories are reflections of a particular world view which, like all other world views, rests on axioms which we do not reflect upon or verbalize because they are to us so natural, right, and proper. Axioms are not akin to Freud's unconscious. They are the distillates of a powerful socialization process that tells us what people are, what the world is, and why we are who and what we are. Axioms are not the sorts of things that are rationally achieved. They are, so to speak, given to us, and we take them as given. That is reason enough for us in *American* psychology to preserve a degree of skepticism towards self-serving centennials. May I conclude by suggesting that psychology has two related missions: to understand America and Americans. If we do that well, we are on the road to understanding people generally.

REFERENCES

BROWN, J. F. 1936. Psychology and the Social Order. McGraw-Hill. New York.
DE TOCQUEVILLE, A. 1945. Democracy in America. Reprint, Vintage Books. New York.
DEWEY, J. 1965. The reflex arc concept in psychology. *In* John Dewey, Philosophy, Psychology, and Social Practice. J. Ratner, Ed. Reprint, Capricorn Books. New York.

DOLLARD, J. 1935. Criteria for the Life History. Yale University Press. New Haven, CT.

DOLLARD, J. [1937] 1957. Caste and Class in a Southern Town. Reprint, Doubleday Anchor Books. Garden City, NY.

SARASON, S. B. 1981. Psychology Misdirected. Free Press. New York.

SARASON, S. B. 1988. The Making of an American Psychologist. Jossey-Bass. San Francisco.

SARASON, S. B. 1989. The lack of an overarching conception in psychology. J. Mind Behav. **3:** 263–279.

SARASON, S. B. 1990. The Challenge of Art to Psychology. Yale University Press. New Haven, CT.

James McKeen Cattell, the New York Academy of Sciences, and the American Psychological Association, 1891-1902

MICHAEL M. SOKAL
Worcester Polytechnic Institute
100 Institute Road
Worcester, Massachusetts 01609-2280

As the 1890s began, New Yorkers and other Americans looked to the future with more optimism than they had for quite some time. For the city and for the country at large, recovery from the Panic of 1877 was at last in sight, and within a few years commentators began to speak of "the Gay Nineties" (Higham 1965). New York itself embarked upon an ambitious program of political consolidation (Hammack 1982) that led to its 1898 merger with the City of Brooklyn to form the City of Greater New York, and many prominent New Yorkers, tired of the city's notorious political machines, supported reform. Buoyed by the success of Seth Low's progressive mayoralities (from 1881 through 1885) in Brooklyn, reformers felt more confident than ever before, and through the following decade and a half New York politics transformed itself. In 1901, progressive elements succeeded in electing Low mayor of the unified city, and several even argued (with more optimism than prescience) that New York's days of corruption had passed (McCormick 1978; Swett 1960).

New York cultural and scientific institutions also thrived through the 1890s, as New Yorkers extended the successes of the previous decade (Bender 1987). The Metropolitan Museum of Art had occupied new buildings in 1880 and 1888 and the new Metropolitan Opera House opened in 1883, and throughout the 1890s both attracted thousands of lovers of art and music (Federal Writers' Project 1939). The American Association for the Advancement of Science had held its annual peripatetic meeting in New York in August 1887, and to prepare for the event (which almost 2,000 attended) New York scientists had worked together as never before (Baatz 1990). In the years that followed, they took advantage of their new cooperative spirit. In a noteworthy effort, scientists and other cultural activists worked through the early 1890s to form, through a merger of three large privately endowed collections, what in 1895 became known as The New York Public Library, Astor, Lenox and Tilden Foundations (Baatz 1990). In response to a call for public support for the new institution, municipal authorities donated land and constructed (from 1902) a magnificent new library building. (Such activity served both traditional politicians, who found sources for patronage in construction contracts, and reformers, who saw the new library as a symbol of their success.) In the same way, between 1889 and 1901, both the city and the state spent about $5 million to expand the buildings of the American Museum of Natural History and, from 1891, the city appropriated about $100 thousand annually for museum salaries and other general expenses (Kennedy 1968; Rainger 1991). New scientific institutions also emerged, as the State Legislature incorporated the New York Botanical Garden in 1891 and the New York Zoological Society opened a new Zoological Park in 1899. Both occupied city-owned land and were maintained with city appropriations, and the Zoological Society extended this tradition in 1902 when it took charge of the New York Aquarium (Federal Writers' Project 1939; Horowitz 1975). No wonder that a contemporaneous European observer of New York culture found these developments "overwhelming" (Meyer 1903, 323).

Universities and colleges in the city also thrived through the 1890s and immediately thereafter, as New York University (NYU) expanded its facilities at Washington Square and established a new campus on University Heights, and from 1903 through 1907 City College also built a new campus. Most notably, perhaps, through the 1890s Columbia College transformed itself from an institution that Henry Adams ridiculed in his Gilded-Age novel *Democracy* (Adams 1878) into one of the country's leading universities (Veysey 1965). Seth Low became its president in 1890, rallied much of the city's cultural and economic leadership behind him, and by the late 1890s had accomplished (partly with his own funds) the institution's removal to a new and larger campus on Morningside Heights. But Columbia's metamorphosis went far beyond the physical, for when its relocation was completed, it had by then established Barnard College for Women, absorbed Teachers College, created several new graduate faculties, and in 1895 formally became Columbia University in the City of New York. Its new Faculty of Political Science, taking its name seriously, supported the municipal research bureaus on which Low's political-reformer allies relied (Karl 1974), and the Faculty of Philosophy soon established itself as a leading graduate school of arts and sciences. This spectacular growth along physical, professional, and intellectual lines established a momentum that carried into the next decade, so that the 1902 inauguration of Low's successor, Nicholas Murray Butler, attracted much favorable attention (FIG. 1). And only eight years later, an astute observer wrote that "Columbia is at present advancing most rapidly and is likely soon to outstrip all the other [American] universities" (Slosson 1910, 524).

Scientists at Columbia, at New York's other colleges and universities, and at the city-supported cultural institutions all found common ground in the

FIGURE 1. Academic procession at the 1902 inauguration of Nicholas Murray Butler as president of Columbia University. Butler and Seth Low (his predecessor) lead the platform party of distinguished guests, including Theodore Roosevelt [far right], then President of the United States. (Courtesy of Columbia University, Columbiana collection.)

New York Academy of Sciences (NYAS). Established in 1817, the Academy through mid-century was struggling through a succession of crises, its goals becoming more and more dubious, but it reemerged in the late 1880s as the center of coordinated planning for the 1887 AAAS meeting. Soon thereafter the Academy began an ambitious program of annual receptions and exhibits designed to bring its members' exciting new science to the public's attention, and through the early 1890s New York newspapers regularly reported on its activities (Baatz 1990).

It also provided the framework for the developments that emerged late in 1890 as the Scientific Alliance of New York. Led by Nathaniel Lord Britton, then Professor of Botany at Columbia and from 1896 Director of the Botanical Garden (for which he had vigorously campaigned), New York scientists saw the Alliance as a center about which local scientific activity could coalesce. And at a time when regional organizations—like the Torrey Botanical Club, the Linnaean Society of New York, and the New York

Mathematical Society—had not yet been superseded by national specialized scientific societies, their forward-looking members saw a real need for the Alliance to fill. Modelled in part after London scientific institutions such as the Royal Society and the Royal Institution, the Alliance represented an attempt to coordinate and promote all scientific activity in the city, and was designed to establish contacts, prevent duplication of effort and, generally, to promote the interests of its member organizations. Britton's plans included a library and meeting rooms for all New York scientists and their societies, and for several years the Alliance issued annual directories of the New York scientific community and weekly bulletins announcing local meetings of interest. Within a few years most major New York scientific societies supported its work and sent representatives to the Council that coordinated its activities. One of the Academy's delegates was Charles F. Cox, a New York Central Railroad executive whose serious amateur interests in geology and Darwinian thought exemplified much of the scientific activity supported by the Alliance's constituent societies. He devoted much time and energy to the Alliance and its programs and eventually became its President. But he never identified himself as a scientist and thus could never support the professional interests of many of his colleagues.

This was the scientific community into which James McKeen Cattell moved in 1891, when he became Professor of Psychology at Columbia. While he and his work remain well-known in late twentieth-century America, his continuing importance among different groups rests on different aspects of his career. For example, most scientists know him primarily as the long-time owner and editor of *Science,* a weekly magazine that was at the point of failure when he took it over in 1894, soon converting it into the country's most important (and widely read) general scientific periodical (Sokal 1980). In 1900, he arranged for *Science* (which remained privately owned) to become the official journal of the American Association for the Advancement of Science, a move that revitalized the AAAS and greatly increased the journal's circulation (and thus its advertising income). Cattell's ties with the AAAS led him to assume a leading role in its affairs quite early in the twentieth century, and he later chaired its Executive Committee for twenty years through the 1920s and 1930s.

Among psychologists, Cattell is revered as the first to use (through the 1890s) German experimental techniques to measure psychological differences between people, and while his tests failed to yield valuable results and were soon abandoned (Sokal 1982), he set the precedent for testing and, perhaps more importantly, for a generally applicable psychology (Sokal 1981b). In the academic community at large, professors remember him for being fired in October 1917 by Nicholas Murray Butler. Although Butler dismissed Cattell ostensibly for his opposition to World War I draft policies, all knowledgeable contemporaneous observers were well aware of the long history of personal and professional animosity between Cattell and many others at Columbia, and the incident soon became one of the country's most celebrated controversies over academic freedom of the period (Gruber 1976). Finally, librarians and sociologists of science know him as the originator (in 1906) of *American Men of Science,* continued today (in an 18th edition just issued) as *American Men and Women of Science.* For Cattell these were not merely *Who's Who* listings, but served primarily as sources of data for his continuing studies of individual differences and, in particular, of the characteristics of scientists (Sokal, forthcoming).

For New Yorkers, however, a historian should emphasize the major roles that Cattell played in the New York scientific community from 1891, when he moved to Columbia, through 1902, when national concerns began absorbing almost all of his attention. Significantly, Cattell's work in this metropolitan community helped shape his attitudes and approaches toward national science policy, and his attempts (for example) to shape the AAAS's response to developments in the American political scene around World War I derive directly from his New York experiences. These in turn were rooted in his earlier life and career, which thus deserve review.

Cattell was born in 1860 and in 1876 entered Lafayette College (see FIGURE 2, Cattell's portrait as a college senior), the fine liberal arts institution in Easton, Pennsylvania, that his father, William C. Cattell, served as President (Sokal 1981a). As a college student, he studied and felt the impact of several aspects of the Positive Philosophy expounded earlier in the century by Auguste Comte, and these ideas deeply influenced him through the following decades. For example, he was drawn initially to Comtean Positivism largely through its ethical teachings, which center around altruism, and derive from Comte's idealization of the sacrifice of mothers in childbirth. With its emphasis on motherhood, this aspect of Comtean thought is often seen as "Catholicism without Christianity," but Cattell drew from it a different message. That is, it reinforced his deep belief (derived from his experiences in childhood) in the centrality of family life (Sokal 1990) and later led him to support programs of positive eugenics that promoted early marriages and large families among scientists and other intellectuals. Of more immediate significance, Comte's emphasis on

FIGURE 2. James McKeen Cattell, 1880, as a college senior. (*Vigintennial Reunion: Class of 1880,* Lafayette College, Easton, PA.)

mathematics impressed him greatly, and many aspects of his later scientific work reflect this influence (Sokal 1981a). Finally, Comte's hierarchy of the sciences, which ran from mathematics to sociology, stirred his interest. But he soon questioned this simple one-dimensional spectrum and throughout the years that followed often rethought the relations among the sciences.

These philosophical concerns led Cattell to study from 1880 through 1882 at the universities of Göttingen and Leipzig, where he learned of the scientific approach to philosophical questions that was then emerging under the name of physiological psychology. At his father's urging, he then applied for and won a fellowship in philosophy at Johns Hopkins University, then the only American institution that offered graduate education in philosophy on a par with Germany's. He studied with such leading American philosophers at George Sylvester Morris and (possibly) Charles Sanders Peirce, and on his own continued his criticisms of Comte's ideas on relations of the sciences (FIGURE 3 presents a fragment of Cattell's notes of 1882–1883 on the relations of the sciences). More importantly, following Comte's emphasis on the authority of science and the new psychologists' appeal to the laboratory, he began to experiment, first in the physiological laboratory established by Johns Hopkins Professor of Biology H. Newell Martin, and then informally, with his classmates, with such drugs as hashish and morphine. His first observation while under their influence—"I seemed to be two persons one of which could observe and even experiment on the other" (Sokal 1981a, 51)—drove home to him the value of the scientific, experimental study of psychology, and in February 1883 he began working in the university's "new physiologico-psychological laboratory" that G. Stanley

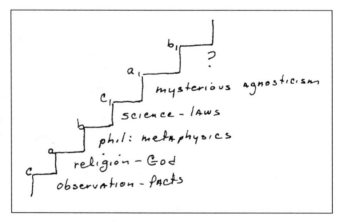

FIGURE 3. A redrawn fragment of Cattell's unpublished notes from 1882–1883, headed "Thought and Being, Philosophy and Science." (James McKeen Cattell papers, Manuscript Division, U.S. Library of Congress, Washington, DC.)

Hall had just opened. He soon extended traditional reaction-time experiments, modifying the standard pieces of apparatus used to conduct them, and obtained highly precise results that both satisfied his Comtean desire for quantitative data and suggested an important new way of understanding the act of reading (Cattell 1885). Despite this success, the university did not renew his fellowship, as Hall apparently misled Hopkins officials as to the value of Cattell's work—even as Hall tried to appropriate it for himself (Ross 1972)—and Cattell's publicly insulting university president Daniel Coit Gilman further aggravated his difficulties (Sokal 1981a).

Leaving Baltimore, Cattell returned to Leipzig, where he worked from 1883 through 1886, nominally under the direction of Wilhelm Wundt, to extend his highly quantitative reaction-time experiments. In doing so, he apparently became the first psychologist to downplay the subject's report of the internal contents and events of his or her mind in favor of observable and measurable behavior—in this case, a subject's precisely determined reaction times under varying conditions (Cattell 1886; Sokal 1981a). Cattell also exhibited a vague and unfocused interest in the individual differences between subjects and their reaction times that his experiments revealed, but he did little beyond mentioning their existence. Unlike Hall, Wundt recognized his student's successes, and named Cattell as his first assistant; in this position, Cattell was able to serve as informal advisor to many other Americans studying in Leipzig. In 1886, despite his German Ph.D., he could not find a teaching position in America, and so looked to England where, from 1886 through 1888 he held a position at St. John's College, Cambridge, with the honorary designation of Fellow Commoner. There and in London he met and talked with leading English intellectuals, and absorbed English attitudes and practices that influenced him throughout his later life. He also established the first Cambridge psychological laboratory (Sokal 1972) and, most importantly, he met and discussed his work with Francis Galton, Darwin's cousin, and one of England's leading promoters of evolutionary ideas. On a personal level, Galton's eugenical call for scientists to have large families resonated with Cattell's Comtean-based belief in the importance of family life and, more scientifically, Galton's overriding concerns with individual differences—the variations that made natural selection possible—gave Cattell a center around which he could focus his previously unformed interest in these differences. In particular, at Galton's London-based anthropometric laboratory, Cattell observed how his English host adapted relatively simple physiological (and even, after his contacts with Cattell, psychological) laboratory procedures to gather data documenting human variation (FIG. 4) (Sokal 1981a). The importance of this experience for Cattell's later career cannot be overstated.

During Cattell's stay in England, his father had the University of Pennsylvania create for him a chair in experimental psychology that, despite his

MR. FRANCIS GALTON'S ANTHROPOMETRIC LABORATORY.

The Laboratory communicates with the Western Gallery containing the Scientific Collections of the South Kensington Museum. Admission to the Gallery is free. It is entered either from Queen's Gate or from Exhibition Road.

Date of Measurement.	Initials.	Birthday. Day. Month.	Sex.	Eye Color.	Single, Married, or Widowed?	Page of Register.
11 Aug 1888	JMcK	25 · 5 · 6.2	m	Grey	Single	626

Head length, maximum from root of nose. Inch. Tenths.	Head breadth maximum. Inch. Tenths.	Height standing, less heels of shoed. Inch. Tenths.	Span of arms from opposite finger tips. Inch. Tenths.	Weight in ordinary clothing. lbs.	Breathing capacity. Cubic inches.	Strength of squeeze. Right hand. lbs. / Left hand. lbs.	Keenness of Eyesight. Distance of reading diamond numerals. Right eye. / Left eye.	Snellen's type read at 20 feet. Inches.	No. of Type	Color Sense.	? Normal.
7	5 8¼	66 7	68·9	144	238	89 82	16	12	218	Yes	? Normal.

Judgment of Eye.

Height of top of knee, when sitting, less heels. Inch. Tenths.	Length of elbow to finger tip left arm. Inch. Tenths.	Length of middle finger of left hand. Inch. Tenths.	Keenness of hearing. ? Normal.	Highest audible note. Vibrations per second.	Reaction time. To sight. Hundredths of a second. / To sound. Hundredths of a second.	Error in dividing a line of 10 inches in half. Per cent.	Error in degrees, estimating an angle of			Height sitting above seat of chair. Inch. Tenths.
21 1	17.7	4·3	Yes	19,000	30 20	0	90° 3	60° 1	10	34 8

One page of the Register is assigned to each person measured, in which his measurements at successive periods are entered in successive lines. No names appear on the Register. The measurements that are entered are those marked with an asterisk ('). Copies of the entries can be obtained through application of the persons measured, or by their representative, under such conditions and restrictions as may be fixed from time to time.

FIGURE 4. The record of James McKeen Cattell's visit to Francis Galton's anthropometric laboratory, London, 11 August 1888. (James McKeen Cattell papers, Manuscript Division, U.S. Library of Congress, Washington, DC.)

later claims, was not the first such professorship in America (Sokal 1981a). In Philadelphia, Cattell worked closely with several colleagues and began two important research programs: a reevaluation of the assumptions underlying classical psychophysics (Fullerton and Cattell 1892), and an attempt to measure more precisely than ever before the velocity of the nervous impulse (Cattell and Dolley 1896). Psychologists continue to cite both analyses today. He also gave well-attended public lectures, began training students (notably Lightner Witmer), and gradually became part of the Philadelphia scientific community, as (for example) a fellow of the American Philosophical Society. Meanwhile, as noted earlier, Columbia University began emerging from Columbia College, and the new Faculty of Philosophy, with Nicholas Murray Butler as its Dean, sought to develop its programs in psychology. In 1890, in an *American Journal of Psychology* review entitled "Psychology at Columbia College," Butler (1890) all but apologized for not having an experimental psychologist on campus, but soon thereafter arranged for Cattell to commute from Philadelphia to teach one day a week at Columbia during the 1890–1891 academic year. Before 1890 closed, Low agreed to double Cattell's University of Pennsylvania salary (to $2,500 annually) and name him Professor of Psychology at Columbia, a position he held through 1917.

Once installed at Columbia, Cattell focused his attention on a major program of psychological tests (FIG. 5) that he had begun, although on a much smaller scale, in Philadelphia, and built a graduate program to support his work (Cattell and Farrand 1896). In New York, he, his junior colleagues (especially Livingston Farrand), and his students—including Edward L. Thorndike, Robert S. Woodworth, Shepherd I. Franz, Frederic L. Wells, among many others—tested all undergraduates at Columbia, as freshman and as seniors, throughout the 1890s, and soon the anthropometric data they had gathered surpassed, in quantity at least, the masses that Galton had collected in England. When asked the value of these data, and indeed of his testing program, Cattell readily admitted that he could not answer definitively. He compared his work with that of early nineteenth-century electrical experiments, who "believed that practical applications would be made, but knew that their first duty was to obtain more exact knowledge." It was his view that "the best way to obtain the knowledge we need is to make more tests, and determine from the results what value they have" (Sokal 1987, 32). But from the start Cattell had great faith in the results of his tests; after all, they were precisely quantitative—for example, he measured reaction times to the millisecond—and he was accordingly confident that they met positivistic criteria for good science. Comte's influence emerged in Cattell's teaching at Columbia and in 1890–1891 his final examination in a first psychology course asked students to "classify the sciences, and subdivide psychology in the way you consider best. Give the subject-

Laboratory of

Psychology of Columbia University

Physical and Mental Tests.

Name_____Date of Birth_____
Birthplace_____of father_____of mother_____
Class_____Profession of father_____
Color of eyes_____of hair_____
Perception of size_____Memory for size_____
Height_____Weight_____

Breathing capacity $\begin{cases} 1\_\_\_\_\_ \\ 2\_\_\_\_\_ \end{cases}$ Size of head_____Right-handed?_____

Strength of hand, right $\begin{cases} 1\_\_\_\_\_ \\ 2\_\_\_\_\_ \end{cases}$ Left $\begin{cases} 1\_\_\_\_\_ \\ 2\_\_\_\_\_ \end{cases}$

Keeness of sight, right eye_____Left_____
Keenness of hearing, right ear_____Left_____

Reaction-time $\Bigg\{$

	1	2	3	4	5	Av.

After-images_____
Color vision_____Perception of pitch_____
Perception of weight 1____2____3____Sensation areas 1____2____3____4____5____

Sensitiveness to pain $\begin{cases} \text{right hand}\_\_\_\_\_ \\ \text{left hand}\_\_\_\_\_ \end{cases}$ Preference for color_____

1	2	3

Perception of time_____
Accuracy of movement_____Rate of perception and movement_____
Memory_____
Imagery_____
Are you willing to repeat these tests at the end of the Sophomore and Senior
years?_____Do you wish to have a copy of these tests sent you?_____
Date of measurement_____Recorded by_____

FIGURE 5. Record-blank used by James McKeen Cattell at Columbia University, ca. 1896. (Cattell, J. M. & L. Farrand. 1896. Physical and mental measurements of students of Columbia University. Psychol. Rev. 3: 618–648.)

matter of your divisions with their relation to one another and to other sciences" (Cattell 1891).

As a Columbia professor, Cattell involved himself in the university's expansion through the 1890s and worked to promote Teachers College, the Department of Philosophy—helping to recruit both John Dewey and Frederick J. E. Woodbridge—and anthropological instruction at Columbia. He helped arrange a university appointment for Museum of Natural History anthropologist Franz Boas, who in the following half century at Columbia built the nation's most influential research and teaching group around his discipline. But even here Cattell's Comtean background played a major role, as Cattell sought Boas, who held a Ph.D. in physics, at least partially for his mathematical expertise. Once Boas joined the Columbia facility, Cattell had him teach his students the mathematics and statistics of correlation, and it was Clark Wissler, one of Cattell's students who later pursued a career in anthropology under Boas's influence, whose 1901 statistical analysis showed that the data Cattell gathered through his tests correlated with nothing (Sokal 1987). This study put an effective end to Cattell's anthropometric testing program, and not until others (like Henry H. Goddard) brought Alfred Binet's more functional tests from France did testing again thrive in America (Zenderland 1987).

Soon after his arrival at Columbia, Cattell helped establish the American Psychological Association, and worked hard to promote its early growth (Sokal 1992). He was one of twenty-six charter members invited by APA founder G. Stanley Hall to an organizational meeting at Clark University in Worcester in July 1892 which, like most other charter members, he probably did not attend. But he was active in the Association from its first annual meeting in December 1892, and especially from 1893, as the APA's second secretary. Most importantly, he compiled and edited the APA's first published proceedings, issued in 1894 (Sokal 1973), and nominated and worked to elect the APA's first women members, Mary Whiton Calkins and Christine Ladd Franklin. His letters on the topic argued that "we psychologists ought not to draw a sex line" (Cattell 1893–94) and his colleagues agreed with him. Cattell also served as the APA's fourth president, after the first generation of leaders (Hall, George T. Ladd, and William James) had been so honored, and chaired the APA's first operating committee, on physical and mental tests. To be sure, this committee achieved few substantive results, as it took (with Cattell, and with most of its other members, including Joseph Jastrow) an anthropometric, rather than a functional, approach to its charge. But that it secured any results at all set it apart from other Association committees whose initiative failed before they could get started (Sokal 1992).

Not surprisingly, Cattell became involved with the New York scientific community soon after he moved to New York. He was elected a resident member of the New York Academy of Sciences on 5 March 1894, and gave his first paper before the Academy, on his Columbia tests, on 27 May 1895 (New York Academy of Sciences 1895). And while he did not join those petitioning for the creation of an Academy Section on Anthropology, Psychology and Philology in November 1895 (McGee, undated; Tobach 1976), he was named to the committee charged by the Academy's Council to review the petition and recommend action. Early in 1896, this committee urged the Council to accept the petition (New York Academy of Sciences 1895–96), and Cattell soon began speaking regularly at its meetings; for example, on 27 April 1896, on "Photometric Difference by Times of Perception" (New York Academy of Sciences 1896). Perhaps more important in his urging his junior colleagues and students to speak at section meetings, and through the late 1890s many Columbia psychologists, including Farrand, Franz, Thorndike, Wissler, and Woodworth all regular addressed its members. In the meantime, the Academy recognized Cattell by naming him a Fellow on 27 February 1899, and electing him chairman of the Section for 1900.

But Cattell's primary activity with the Academy through the 1890s involved its annual receptions and exhibits, the success of which brought science before the city's educated public (Baatz 1990). Throughout the decade they attracted many attendees, received extensive coverage in the local press, and such national journals as *Scientific American* and *Science* gave them much attention (New York Academy of Sciences 1896). In all, their success illustrated the Academy's growth and reputation in the years immediately before the century's end, and reinforced its members' optimism. At the first exhibit, held in 1894 at the Library of Columbia College, Cattell took charge of the Department of Experimental Psychology, and arranged for exhibits of (among other things) the instruments he used for his Columbia tests of color vision and the perception of weight. His announcement emphasized that "visitors are invited to use the instruments exhibited, with each of which will be found instructions and blanks for making records" (New York Academy of Sciences 1894, 13), and in this way he followed the precedent of Galton's anthropometric laboratory in London quite closely. The success of this event led the Academy to move the Second Annual Exhibit to larger quarters—the Gallery of the American Fine Arts Society—where Cattell's junior colleague, Livingston Farrand, took charge of the psychological material, with the assistance of their students S. I. Franz and Harold Griffing (New York Academy of Sciences 1895). In 1896 and 1897, Cattell again oversaw the exhibits, and displayed instruments used in his laboratory and in those of his friends Edward W. Scripture of Yale and Charles Bliss of NYU (New York Academy of Sciences 1896; 1897), and his students often first discussed their work in public at such Academy events.

But in the years that followed, Bliss, Thorndike, and Charles H. Judd (Bliss's successor at NYU) took charge of these exhibits, as national concerns began to occupy more and more of Cattell's attention and, as an "entrepreneur of science" and editor of major national scientific journals, he began spending more time on what we now call "science policy" than he did on science itself. In 1894, he and James Mark Baldwin of Princeton founded and began editing the *Psychological Review*, in part to counter the influence of Hall's *American Journal of Psychology* (Sokal 1992). In 1894, he purchased *Science*, which under his editorship became the country's most important general scientific journal (Sokal 1980). He chose an editorial board of "leading American men of science" whose names he proudly displayed on *Science*'s masthead, listing them in the order of Comte's hierarchy of the sciences (FIGURE 6 shows *Science*'s first editorial board). But even as he moved onto the national stage, Cattell continued his interest in New York science, and began using *Science* as a platform from which to promote its interests, especially Britton's and Cox's program for the Scientific Alliance. From the start of Cattell's editorship, the journal regularly published proceedings of Academy meetings in abstract (New York Academy of Sciences 1895; 1896), long articles on NYAS annual exhibits (Wade 1896), and from the mid-1890s, especially detailed reports on plans and activities of the Scientific Alliance began to appear, for example, "A Proposed Building for the Scientific Alliance of New York" (1898), "The Scientific Alliance of New York" (1899; 1901), and "Research Funds of the Scientific Alliance of New York" (1903). Throughout this period, *Science* supported Britton's and Cox's proposals editorially ("A Building for the Scientific Societies of New York," 1896), and Cattell often discussed with Britton and Cox how best to raise funds for the Alliance, and to report in *Science* gifts from J. P. Morgan and other major benefactors; the philanthropy of a benefactor like Esther Hermann, for instance, is noted in Britton, Cattell, and Cox, 1899–1903.

By the turn of the century, national concerns demanded more of Cattell's attention, but he still reported New York activities in *Science* even as he took over *Popular Science Monthly* in 1900 and was elected to the National Academy of Sciences in 1901. In the following year, Cattell's journals began to support the campaign for Convocation Week, with its plans for joint meetings of all major U.S. scientific societies during the week between Christmas and New Year's Day (Sokal 1980), an effort endorsed by the American Association for the Advancement of Science that followed the tradition of the American Society of Naturalists (Appel 1988). At the same time, Cattell refocused his scientific work on what he called "the natural history of American men of science" in a project that culminated in his *American Men of Science* directories. As noted, this program was for him primarily a study of individual differences among scientists, and between scientists and others,

SCIENCE

A WEEKLY JOURNAL

DEVOTED TO THE ADVANCEMENT OF SCIENCE.

EDITORIAL COMMITTEE : S. NEWCOMB, Mathematics ; R. S. WOODWARD, Mechanics ; E. C. PICKERING, Astronomy ; T. C. MENDENHALL, Physics ; R. H. THURSTON, Engineering ; IRA REMSEN, Chemistry ; J. LE CONTE, Geology; W. M. DAVIS, Physiography; O. C. MARSH, Paleontology; W. K. BROOKS, Invertebrate Zoölogy ; C. HART MERRIAM, Vertebrate Zoölogy ; S. H. SCUDDER, Entomology ; N. L. BRITTON, Botany ; HENRY F. OSBORN, General Biology ; H. P. BOWDITCH, Physiology ; J. S. BILLINGS, Hygiene ; J. MCKEEN CATTELL, Psychology ; DANIEL G. BRINTON, J. W. POWELL, Anthropology.

NEW SERIES. VOLUME I.

JANUARY TO JUNE, 1895.

NEW YORK
41 EAST FORTY-NINTH STREET
1895

FIGURE 6. Title page of the first volume of *Science* edited by James McKeen Cattell.

and it attracted funding from the Carnegie Institution of Washington (which awarded Cattell its grant no. 2) and from the Scientific Alliance's Esther Hermann Fund.

In 1902, Cattell also served as president of both the New York Academy of Sciences and of the American Society of Naturalists; these positions demonstrated his growing stature and his ongoing scientific and political concerns, and, so far from being merely ceremonial posts, demanded much attention throughout the year. These demands peaked in December 1902, and culminated during Convocation Week in Washington, DC, where he established an anthropometric laboratory to collect physical and physiological data from the scientists attending their meetings, thus continuing his (and Galton's) earlier anthropometric studies. That month he had to deliver presidential addresses to each group, and these addresses demonstrate effectively just how his political positions and his scientific interests both derived largely from his earlier concerns for the relations among the sciences and also, most interestingly, from his experiences with the New York scientific community. They also illustrate how these experiences helped shaped his view of the national scientific community.

Entitled "Homo Scientificus Americanus" (Cattell 1903), Cattell's presidential address before the American Society of Naturalists was delivered in Washington on 1 January 1903. Cattell described it as his first report on "the natural history of American men of science," and it thus presented data on their education, interests, geographical, and topical distribution. It also included a "graphical representation of the relations of the sciences" (FIGURE 7). Interestingly, this illustration does not appear in the posthumous edition of Cattell's collected papers (Poffenberger 1947). While obviously derived from Comtean considerations, it went beyond Comte's one-dimensional spectrum to emphasize a range of interdependencies, and Cattell found it a tool to help him understand the relationship among scientists and their work. More importantly, it revealed the nature of his larger plans for the national scientific community, whose organization would reflect this logical structure of the sciences. And these plans appear even more clearly in his presidential address to the New York Academy of Sciences.

Cattell had presented this talk two weeks earlier, in New York of course. He entitled it "The Academy of Sciences" (Cattell 1902b) and opened it by reviewing the history of word "academy," the emergence of universities in Europe and America, and the development of scientific societies since the Scientific Revolution. More significantly, Cattell emphasized the relatively recent growth of specialized disciplinary scientific societies, especially in the United States, and described them as "a necessary result of the differentiation of science and the increase of scientific men" (p. 970). At the same time, he noted that their emergence challenged the leadership of more general societies. He then focused his discussion by discussing in some detail the New

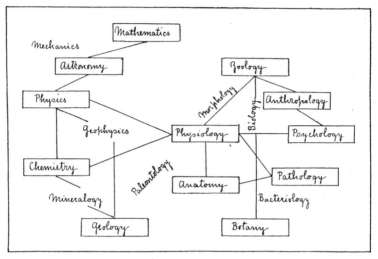

CHART SHOWING THE RELATIONS OF THE SCIENCES.

FIGURE 7. James McKeen Cattell's "graphical representation of the relations of the sciences." (Cattell 1903)

York scientific community and its expansion during the previous decade. In doing so, he characterized the New York Academy of Sciences as the most general society, but stressed its direct connections with the many more specialized local societies and other major New York scientific institutions, and its less direct links with them through the Scientific Alliance of New York. He continually emphasized the value of coordination and cooperation, but illustrated (FIG. 8) how the geographical dispersion of these institutions made very close cooperation impossible. He also noted, almost in passing, that "fifteen years ago the city had a great opportunity" to situate its scientific and other institutions to best effect. Illustrating his vision of what might have been in diagrammatic form (FIG.9), he claimed that, had New York implemented such a plan or one like it, the institutions would have effectively avoided duplication of libraries and other facilities, "and there would have been a strengthening through cooperation for which it is not easy to find words" (p. 971).

But Cattell's presidential address was more than a review of lost opportunities, and he argued that much more could still be done. He thus issued a call for action, emphasizing the coordination of activities of all New York scientific institutions, including universities, research establishments, and societies, with a central organization serving the entire community. He proceeded to propose that this organization could support—perhaps at the American Museum of Natural History—a clubhouse, a library, meeting rooms, and archives, and concluded that "it is immaterial whether the institution be called the New York Academy of Sciences or the Scientific Alliance of New York" (p. 972). New York scientists and others responded most positively to this aspect of Cattell's talk: Cox, for example, wrote to him four days later to praise him for "stirr[ing] up again with zeal for the object I have had before my mind for ten years past,—the efficient cooperation of all the scientific organizations in his city" (Britton, Cattell, and Cox, 1899–1903; 19 December 1902). Cox further agreed that the Academy should adopt the Scientific Alliance's purpose, and in fact the Academy did absorb the Alliance in 1907. To be sure, others shared Cattell's perspective on the issues at hand (Baatz 1990), but his address served an important catalytic function.

Cattell's address went further, however, for he went on to present his general analysis and plans for the national scientific community. As he argued:

The organization of science in America toward which I believe we are moving is this: We shall have a national society for each of the sciences; these societies will be affiliated and will form the American Association for the Advancement of Science, which will hold migratory meetings. Winter meetings will be held in large centers where all the societies will come together, and summer meetings will be held at points of educational and other interest when the societies will scatter somewhat. The council of the American Association

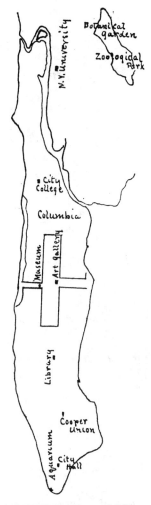

FIGURE 8. James McKeen Cattell's map of New York scientific and cultural institutions in 1902 (Cattell 1902b).

composed of delegates from all the societies will be our chief deliberative and legislative body. Our national societies will consist of local sections, and these sections will unite to form an academy of sciences. The men who are in one neighborhood and engaged in the same kind of work are the natural unit. They should unite on the one hand with those in other neighborhoods to form a national society; they should join on the other

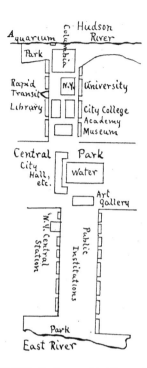

FIGURE 9. James McKeen Cattell's vision of a ideal arrangement for New York scientific and cultural institutions in 1902 (Cattell 1902b).

hand with the men of science of the same neighborhood to form an academy of sciences. This plan of organization may appear to be almost too logical for a world that is somewhat careless of logic, but it is in part already realized. It will in my opinion result as a necessary condition from the state of affairs. Our academy has already contributed to it, and it seems to me that we should continue to do consciously what we have hitherto done rather blindly (pp. 972–973.).

To be sure, Cattell derived the perspectives on science and its organization embodied in this statement from sources beyond those emphasized here. For example, they reflected his belief in the value of the full range of sciences, that is, not just large-scale physical and biomedical science, but also natural history and what have come to be called the social and behavioral sciences. This attitude derived both from Cattell's late nineteenth-century experiences as a pioneer psychologist who had at times to argue for the validity of his science, and also from his education at Lafayette College, which had been rooted in an earlier nineteenth-century approach to science that could identify his statistical studies of the scientific community as a "natural history of American men of science" (Sokal 1990). This statement also reflected his respect for the average scientist, and his work with and the leadership roles he played in both specialized and general national scientific societies, like the American Psychological Association and the American Association for the Advancement of Science. But the influence of his studies of Comtean Positivism and his experiences in New York that appear clearly in this statement and helped coalesce his attitudes thus shaped the course of Cattell's later scientific career.

To speak most generally, then, while Cattell worked with the APA in later years, he remained more devoted to the AAAS, a broader-based institution, which remained under Cattell's leadership the most accessible American scientific society. In the same way, he opened his journals—

especially *Science, Popular Science Monthly,* and its successor, *The Scientific Monthly*—to all sciences and all scientists, and readers of both journals knew that while the biological was always emphasized over the physical, this imbalance did not stem from any bias on Cattell's part. These inclusivist attitudes also influenced Cattell's specific actions at various times during his career; three brief examples can serve to illustrate this point, although many more can be chosen from the full range of his activities during the following forty years. For instance, earlier in 1902, when Andrew Carnegie donated $10 million to found the Carnegie Institution of Washington (CIW), Cattell campaigned in *Science* for a broad-based institution providing grant support for, and opening its laboratories to, scientists across the United States (Cattell 1902a). The Carnegie trustees chose, however, to follow a different route, and the CIW focused its attention on such archetypical examples of what soon would become known as Big Science at its Mount Wilson Observatory, directed by George Ellery Hale, later of the California Institute of Technology and its Geophysical Observatory (Kohler 1991; Reingold 1968; Sokal 1980).

Similarly, more than a decade later, as American academic scientists sought to promote "preparedness" in the years before their country entered World War I, Cattell supported the AAAS Committee of One Hundred on Scientific Research as a "democratic" alternative to the program supported by the National Academy of Sciences and led by Hale that had by 1916 resulted in the creation of the National Research Council. In early 1917 a compromise organizational plan emerged—it might have been drawn directly from Cattell's 1900 address, "The Academy of Sciences"—and involved discipline-based national committees with representatives from the AAAS, the National Research Council (NRC), and the appropriate specialized scientific societies. But the NRC soon coöpted most AAAS delegates, and in the aftermath of Cattell's dismissal from Columbia he and his alternative scheme lost whatever influence they might have had (Plotkin 1978). As might be expected, Cattell reacted bitterly to his dismissal, and in the years that followed, his bitterness only increased (Sokal 1971), especially as the National Academy and its Research Council gained in influence, while the stature of the AAAS steadily declined (Sokal 1980). In 1922, Cattell wrote and circulated among friends a review entitled "The Organization of Scientific Men" that many found extremely funny, and others thought libelous. Before publishing it, he toned down some of its criticisms, both implied and explicit, of Hale and the institutions with which he was identified, but even its published version (Cattell 1922) pulled few punches. For example, he claimed that

[w]hether the Research Council belongs to the National Academy or the National Academy belongs to the Research Council, or both are satellites

of Pasadena is a problem of three bodies that is difficult of solution. The American Association still belongs to its twelve thousand members. (P. 576).

And while he never explicitly cited the plans he had set forth in 1900 for the New York scientific community as an alternative to Hale's, they clearly still determined his perceptions more than twenty years later.

One can argue that failure characterized Cattell's scientific career, and can support this conclusion by citing—to mention only the points discussed in this paper—his anthropometric testing program, his dismissal from Columbia University, and his never-implemented plans for a national scientific community. Certainly his last years were filled with bitterness (Sokal 1971). But Cattell did leave late twentieth-century scientists and others with at least a few things of value. Certainly few of us can survive as scientists and scholars without reading *Science* regularly. And while he focused his attention on the New York Academy of Sciences for only a few years, he did do much to direct its course through the early twentieth century, and from this work we all have benefited. Few of those about whom we write today have done so much.

REFERENCES

ADAMS, H. [1878] 1961. Democracy. Paperback edition. Doubleday. Garden City, NY.

APPEL, T. A. 1988. Organizing biology: The American Society of Naturalists and its "Affiliated Societies." *In* The American Development of Biology, R. Rainger, K. R. Benson, & J. Maienschein, Eds.: 87–120. University of Pennsylvania Press. Philadelphia.

BAATZ, S. 1990. Knowledge, Culture, and Science in the Metropolis: The New York Academy of Sciences, 1817–1970. Ann. N.Y. Acad. Sci. **584:** 1–269.

BENDER, T. 1987. New York Intellect: A History of Intellectual Life in New York City from 1750 to the Beginnings of Our Own Time. Alfred A. Knopf. New York.

BRITTON, N. L. J. M. CATTELL, & C. F. COX. Correspondence relating to the Scientific Alliance of New York, 1899–1903. James McKeen Cattell papers, Manuscript Division, U.S. Library of Congress, Washington. DC.

A building for the scientific societies of New York. *Science* **4:** 686–687.

BUTLER, N. M. 1890. Psychology at Columbia College. Am. J. Psychol. **3:** 277–278.

CATTELL, J. M. 1885. Über die Zeit der Erkennung und Benennung von Schriftzeichen, Bildern und Farben. Philosophische Studien **2:** 635–650.

CATTELL, J. M. 1886. Psychometrische Untersuchungen. Philosophische Studien **3:** 305–335, 452–492.

CATTELL, J. M. 1891. Unpublished final examination, Columbia College. James McKeen Cattell papers, Manuscript Division, U.S. Library of Congress, Washington, DC.

CATTELL, J. M. Unpublished letterbook, 1893–94. James McKeen Cattell papers, Manuscript Division, U.S. Library of Congress, Washington, DC.
CATTELL, J. M. & C. S. DOLLEY. 1896. On reaction-times and the velocity of the nervous impulse. Proc. Nat. Acad. Sci. 7: 393–415.
CATTELL, J. M. 1902a. The Carnegie Institution of Washington. Science 16: 460–469.
CATTELL, J. M. 1902b. The Academy of Sciences. Science 16: 965–974.
CATTELL, J. M. 1903. Homo Scientificus Americanus. Science 17: 561–570.
CATTELL, J. M. 1922. The organization of scientific men. Sci. Monthly 14: 567–577.
CATTELL, J. M. & L. FARRAND. 1896. Physical and mental measurements of students of Columbia University. Psychol. Rev. 3: 618–648.
FEDERAL WRITERS' PROJECT, WORKS PROGRESS ADMINISTRATION. 1939. New York City Guide. Random House. New York.
FULLERTON, G. S. & J. M. CATTELL. 1892. On the Perception of Small Differences: With Special Reference to the Extent, Force, and Time of Movement. University of Pennsylvania. Philadelphia.
GRUBER, C. S. 1976. Mars and Minerva: World War I and the Uses of the Higher Learning in America. Louisiana State University Press. Baton Rouge, LA.
HAMMACK, D. C. 1982. Power and Society: Greater New York at the Turn of the Century. Russell Sage Foundation. New York.
HIGHAM, J. 1965. The reorientation of American culture in the 1890's. In the Origins of Modern Consciousness. J. Weiss, Ed.: 25–48. Wayne State University Press. Detroit, MI.
HOROWITZ, H. L. 1975. Animal and man in the New York Zoological Park. N. Y. Hist. 55: 426–453.
KARL, B. 1974. Charles E. Merriam and the Study of Politics. University of Chicago Press. Chicago.
KENNEDY, J. M. 1968. Philanthropy and science in New York City: The American Museum of Natural History, 1868–1968. Ph.D. dissertation, Yale University. New Haven, CT.
KOHLER, R. E. 1991. Partners in Science: Foundations and Natural Scientists, 1900–1945. University of Chicago Press. Chicago.
McCORMICK, R. L. 1978. Prelude to Progressivism: The transformation of New York State politics, 1890–1910. N. Y. Hist. 59: 253–276.
McGEE, J. P. Psychology and anthropology at the New York Academy of Sciences. Unpublished paper, Department of Psychology, Fordham University. New York. Undated.
MEYER, A. B. 1903. Studies of the museums and kindred institutions of New York City, Albany, Buffalo, and Chicago; I. The City of New York. In Report of the U.S. National Museum, under the Direction of the Smithsonian Institution. Pp. 321–392.
THE NEW YORK ACADEMY OF SCIENCES, 1894. First Annual Reception and Exhibit.
THE NEW YORK ACADEMY OF SCIENCES, 1895. Second Annual Reception and Exhibit.
THE NEW YORK ACADEMY OF SCIENCES, 1895–96. Minutes of the Council.
THE NEW YORK ACADEMY OF SCIENCES, 1896. Third Annual Reception and Exhibit.
THE NEW YORK ACADEMY OF SCIENCES, 1897. Fourth Annual Reception and Exhibit.
THE NEW YORK ACADEMY OF SCIENCES, 1898. Fifth Annual Reception and Exhibit.
THE NEW YORK ACADEMY OF SCIENCES, 1895. Science 1: 727–728.
THE NEW YORK ACADEMY OF SCIENCES, 1896. Science 3: 750–751.

PLOTKIN, H. 1978. Edward C. Pickering and the endowment of scientific research in America. Isis **69:** 44–57.

POFFENBERGER, A. T., Ed. 1947. James McKeen Cattell: Man of Science. 2 vols. Science Press. New York.

A proposed building for the Scientific Alliance of New York. 1898. Science **7:** 408–413.

RAINGER, R. 1991. An Agenda for Antiquity: Henry Fairfield Osborn and Vertebrate Paleontology at the American Museum of Natural history, 1890–1935. University of Alabama Press. Tuscaloosa, AL.

REINGOLD, N. 1968. National aspirations and local purposes. Trans. Kansas Acad. Sci. **71:** 235–246.

Research funds of the Scientific Alliance of New York. 1903. Science **17:** 314–315.

ROSS, D. G. 1972. Stanley Hall: The Psychologist as Prophet. University of Chicago Press. Chicago.

The Scientific Alliance of New York. 1899. Science **9:** 550–551.

The Scientific Alliance of New York. 1901. Science **13:** 596–597.

SLOSSON, E. E. 1910. Great American Universities. Macmillan. New York.

SOKAL, M. M. 1971. The unpublished autobiography of James McKeen Cattell. Am. Psychol. **26:** 626–635.

SOKAL, M. M. 1972. Psychology at Victorian Cambridge—The unofficial laboratory of 1887–1888. Proc. Am. Phil. Soc. **116:** 145–147.

SOKAL, M. M. 1973. APA's first publication: Proceedings of the American Psychological Association, 1892–1893. Am. Psychol. **28:** 277–292.

SOKAL, M. M. 1980. *Science* and James McKeen Cattell, 1894–1945. Science **209:** 43–52.

SOKAL, M. M., Ed. 1981a. An Education in Psychology: James McKeen Cattell's Journal and Letters from Germany and England, 1880–1888. MIT Press. Cambridge, MA.

SOKAL, M. M. 1981b. The origins of The Psychological Corporation. J. Hist. Behav. Sci. **17:** 54–67.

SOKAL, M. M. 1982. James McKeen Cattell and the failure of anthropometric mental testing, 1890–1901. *In* The Problematic Science: Psychology in Nineteenth-Century Thought. W. R. Woodward & M. G. Ash, Eds.: 322–345. Praeger. New York.

SOKAL, M. M., Ed. 1987. Psychological Testing and American Society, 1890–1930. Rutgers University Press. New Brunswick, NJ.

SOKAL, M. M. 1990. Life-span developmental psychology and the history of science. *In* Beyond History of Science: Essays in Honor of Robert E. Schofield. E. W. Garber, Ed.: 67–80. Lehigh University Press. Bethlehem, PA.

SOKAL, M. M. 1992. Origins and early years of the American Psychological Association. Am. Psychol. **47:** 111–122.

SOKAL, M. M. Stargazing: James McKeen Cattell, *American Men of Science,* and the reward structure of the American scientific community, 1906–1944. *In* Psychology, Science, and Human Affairs: Essays in Honor of William Bevan. F. Kessel, Ed. Westview Press. Boulder, CO. In press.

SWETT, S. C. 1960. The test of a reformer: A study of Seth Low, New York City Mayor, 1902–1903. N.-Y. Hist. Soc. Quart. **44:** 5–41.

TOBACH, E. 1976. A brief history of the Psychology Section of the New York Academy of Sciences. Ann. N. Y. Acad. Sci. **270:** 6–13.

VEYSEY, L. 1965. The Emergence of the American University. University of Chicago Press. Chicago.

WADE, H. T. 1896. Annual Reception and Exhibition of the New York Academy of Sciences. Science **3**: 507–509.

ZENDERLAND, L. 1987. The debate over diagnosis: Henry Herbert Goddard and the medical acceptance of intelligence testing. *In* Psychological Testing and American Society, 1890–1930. M. M. Sokal, Ed.: 46–74. Rutgers University Press. New Brunswick, NJ.

An Epistemological Critique of Experimentalism in Psychology; or, Why G. Stanley Hall Waited Until William James Was Out of Town to Found the American Psychological Association

EUGENE TAYLOR

Department of Psychiatry
Harvard Medical School
Boston, Massachusetts 02115

William James was away in Europe on that hot summer day in July when the first meeting of the American Psychological Association (APA) convened in G. Stanley Hall's parlor at Clark University. Was this by accident or by design? We know, on the one hand, that James was acknowledged as a psychologist of consequence by those present because he was elected a charter member *in absentia*. On the other, the only inkling we have of James's reaction comes from an inquiry that Fernberger had put to James McKeen Cattell in 1942 about the matter. Cattell responded only that "James was not at the beginning very favorable to the organization" (Fernberger 1943, 35).

One can only speculate what Cattell had meant. The relationship between James and Hall began in collegial friendship in the first years after they met in 1876, but by 1892 they had become combative and distant, although still respectful of one another, largely over issues related to their distinctly different visions of psychology as a science. Certainly this developing estrangement must have played a role in Hall's actions and in James's response, and so might profitably reward investigation. As well, Cattell's remark could also possibly reflect James's rising militancy, both before and after 1892, toward bigness in general, the founding of institutions designed to erect boundaries between the disciplines, the pretensions of exact laboratory science, and what James referred to as blatant trade unionism in the helping professions.

These, and other factors only now emerging from new scholarly work, conspired to place James and Hall in their respective positions in 1892. The result, at least from James's perspective, was not entirely negative, for, despite his original misgivings about the enterprise, his election to the presidency of the APA in 1894 presented him with an unprecedented opportunity to introduce a potential means by which psychologists could periodically renovate their new science.

JAMES AND HALL

When Hall arrived as a graduate student in the fall of 1876 to study the new psychology under Assistant Professor William James, Harvard University was the only place in America where scientific laboratory methods were being taught at that time. We are not exactly sure whether this was Hall's primary motive in coming, for even then, as judged by his later biographers, Hall was an enigmatic character, uncertain of his future direction, and prone to a profound ambivalence of thought. As Dorothy Ross (1972, xiv) has characterized him, he was at once late Victorian and post-Darwinian:

His rhetoric and his work were permeated with both religion and science. His evolutionary theories were simultaneously tied to outdated biological concepts of the race as well as more sophisticated ideas of nature-nurture. He wanted to be both the village preacher and cosmopolitan man of science. He had a canny sense for the underside of every idea, the ambivalence that lurked behind every belief, and he often managed to profess both sides of a question at once.

In many respects, Hall well represented the transition from the old to the new era. But the prevailing view among historians is that, despite the brilliance and erudition he displayed in all of his future accomplishments in psychology, in the end, Hall was the victim of his own duplicity, self-absorption, and mean dealing.

It would not be stretching the point too far to say that at the heart of Hall's failure to lead in the new psychology was his paradoxical relationship with William James. From the first, James's approach to Hall was that of a cordial ally, an attitude that only engendered in Hall an ever-increasing competitive hostility, for Hall always presumed he was equal to James's accomplishments (Ross, 1972, 65; Perry 1935, vol. 1, 155–164, 169–177, 181, 202–209, 228–230, 507, 533–534).

JAMES AND HALL ON THE NEW PHILOSOPHY

This struggle for ascendancy over James commenced virtually the week classes began at Harvard for the fall semester of 1876. Just then Hall's letter

"College Instruction in Philosophy" appeared in *The Nation*, preceded by a lengthy comment by William James on the same topic. Hall had evidently written to the editor first, wishing that *The Nation* would devote some space to the condition of philosophical education in American colleges. Having visited "the class-rooms of many of our best institutions," Hall believed himself adequate to the task of critiquing what was so inadequately taught as philosophy. The problem, as he saw it, was that marvelous new developments in England and Germany, such as the application of scientific methods in psychology by Spencer, Lewes, Lotze, and Wundt, and admirable textbooks accessible in the history of philosophy, were being completely ignored, as was the application of philosophy to law, politics, and education. Instead, American colleges taught Hamilton, Butler, and a score of other texts on mental science that were mere apologies for theological dogma. The general aim of all philosophic education, Hall concluded, should be to teach how to think, and not simply tell the students what to think. Hall did mention one exception, however—that recent lectures at Harvard on the modern systems of philosophy show what can be accomplished.

Instigated by Hall's letter, the editors had also approached James, who responded with a statement four times longer than Hall's. However, being the more substantive, James's article was placed first in the more prestigious Notes section. Hall's letter, in contrast, appeared in the back of the journal under Correspondence.

James opened his piece by vigorously agreeing with a recent author whom he referred to only as "G.S.H." The point of agreement was that, when philosophy was only taught by the college president, who may have an excellent character but few speculative gifts, the students lose mental perspective:

> However sceptical one may be of the attainment of universal truths (and to make our position more emphatic, we are willing here to concede the extreme Positivistic position), one can never deny that philosophic study means the habit of always seeing an alternative, of not taking the usual for granted, of making conventionalities fluid again, of imagining foreign states of mind. (James 1876, 178)

If colleges are to produce men and not machines, James said, then they should look well at this aspect of their influence.

But James took umbrage with the opposite extreme as well. Adherents of the new science were all talking about Fechner and Helmholtz, as if some single observation in psychophysics was all that important psychologically. Science was the vogue, but most people were unprepared to understand it. In particular, one cannot criticize the new developments unless thoroughly grounded in physiology. He concluded by citing McCosh, traditionalist, moral philosopher, and president of Princeton, who said that philosophers cannot abandon metaphysics to those trained solely in the new sciences. Rather, philosophers should themselves take up the study of physiology, conduct research, and master the ascertained facts. In short, the philosopher "must not give up the study of the nervous system and brain to those who cannot comprehend anything beyond . . . their senses."

Finally, as if he had not fully read Hall's coda, James pointed out that at Harvard, one could study Locke, Kant, Schopenhauer, Hartmann, Hodgson, and Spencer. This meant, James said, that the complaint of "universal academic stagnation" in American universities was not wholly justified.

We are not completely in the dark concerning what effect these publications must have had on Hall's entrance into the Harvard community. As James later wrote, they were taken somewhat negatively. It was clear that Hall had a much more inflated opinion of himself than did the Harvard Overseers, who saw him as a mere instructor (he taught English his first year), and a graduate student at that. James, however, welcomed him cordially, gave him free run of what laboratory facilities were available, put him in contact with Henry Pickering Bowditch, and introduced him around the local philosophical circles.[a]

HALL'S EXPERIMENTS AT HARVARD

Hall apparently threw himself into his teaching duties the first year with total absorption, as the Harvard Library Charging Records show he checked out works exclusively on the classics and literature during 1876–1877, all subjects entirely commensurate with his task as an instructor in English. As early as the summer of 1877, however, once his formal teaching duties in English were complete, he immediately turned his attention to the literature of the new science—Helmholtz, Hering, Lotze, Fechner, and Wundt. In the fall of 1877, he was apparently working full time as a graduate student in philosophy, mixing the new science and German idealism with the older American moral philosophy, and dabbling at the same time in experimental physiology.

Evidence for the activities of graduate students in this early period of Harvard's development of the School of Arts and Sciences is scant, but we do know that sometime between the summer and the fall of 1877 Hall began research into some problems of color perception in Bowditch's physiological laboratory at the Medical School, and that his studies had sufficiently pro-

---

[a]Hall's biographer implies that Hall was influenced by the functional and pragmatic movement in Cambridge during the 1870s. He was remembered in Cambridge circles as a "queer genius" (Ross 1972, 77fn).

gressed to permit him to deliver a formal report to the Boston Society of Medical Sciences in November (1877). Hall there gave a somewhat obtuse discussion of the prevailing color theory based on the differential activation of three sets of cones. He presented evidence from optical illusions and color after-image studies showing that the perception of colors may be distinguished in different planes of the retina. The discussion that followed among the physicians gave Hall mixed reviews. One doctor was interested because he had previously conducted photographic experiments with light and could follow Hall's arguments. Several others merely expressed regret at not having had a chance to review the paper beforehand.

This lecture was apparently practice for the opportunity that came four months later, in March 1878, when Hall presented a fuller account of his work on color perception. This time he spoke to the more prestigious audience of the American Academy of Arts and Sciences, an opportunity probably arranged by James and Bowditch, who were both members.

Hall conducted other investigations, as well, with the help of both James and Bowditch. In 1878 James had availed himself of the opportunity to observe Miss Laura Bridgman, a 44-year-old deaf, blind mute at the Perkins School for the Blind, whose innate intelligence and curiosity had been awakened and developed by Samuel Gridley Howe. Bridgman's life and Howe's accomplishments had been acclaimed by audiences the world over for more than thirty years. (See, for instance, James 1878).

Hall also made some extensive observations of Laura Bridgman which were intended as a part of his dissertation.[b] His account is particularly interesting for several reasons. First, he ran extensive psychophysical tests on this subject, some with equipment supplied by Bowditch. Second, Hall's narrative reveals how closely he adhered to a mechanistic interpretation of consciousness, even though certain facts about Laura's memories and dreams seemed to call this interpretation into question. Third, his account of Bridgman represents the earliest and most detailed single case study of developmental influences in childhood to appear in Hall's bibliographic corpus. One could call it Hall's first excursion in print into what would later be referred to as the genetic method.

While his physiological and psychophysical researchers were proceeding, Hall also continued to pursue interests in philosophy that would eventually become part of his dissertation. "Notes on Hegel and His Critics" appeared in January 1978, in William T. Harris's *Journal of Speculative Philosophy*. Here, following the interpretations of his former teacher Trendelenberg,

---

[b]See Hall (1879). The last part of Hall's dissertation, "The Perception of Space," meant to be Part One of his master plan, refers to his observations of Bridgman as a third section of Part Two. Parts Two and Three were never completed in dissertation form, but sections of them eventually appeared in print as separate articles.

Hall examined Hegel's view on the origin of space perception and his arguments for pure thought from the standpoint of logic and phenomenology. For Hegel, pure thought was all, the most real of all realities. The logic of pure thought was the world in which consciousness lives and moves. Hall's conclusion was that Hegel made for good mental discipline, the best embodiment of the legitimate aspirations of the philosophic sentiment, but was fatal as a final doctrine, and "almost valueless" as a method.

James's own pejorative comment on Hegel was that his universal philosophy reminded him of one of those floozie hotels in Swansy, Massachusetts, that had no private bathrooms. In his essay "On Some Hegelisms" (James 1882), he found the doctrine of the identity of contradictories somewhat absurd, and remarked that Hegel's system reminded him of the type of revelation of eternal truth that one finds under nitrous oxide intoxication.

HALL'S DISSERTATION

In June 1878, Hall was granted the Ph.D. in philosophy at Harvard (Overseer's Records 1871–1882). It is almost universally accepted that this was the first Ph.D. to be granted in America in the so-called new psychology. Supposedly, Hall's dissertation had as its topic the muscular perception of space and was based upon laboratory investigations performed under Bowditch[c]. A close look at Hall's text, however, suggests another interpretation altogether.[d]

In the first place, the dissertation title is not "The Muscular Perception of Space," but "the Perception of Space."[e] It is a polemic argument for empiricism over against philosophical speculation, and although there are references to scientific research, nowhere in the text is there any reference to laboratory experiments Hall himself had conducted. The theoretical thrust of Hall's argument is a blend of messianic Christian rhetoric and American

[c]See the statement by Miles and Miles (1929). Harper (1949) lists Hall as the first Ph.D. of this sort, but Peter Behrens (1986) at Pennsylvania State University has contested this point, claiming that the first Ph.D. in the new scientific laboratory psychology was conferred upon Joseph Jastrow, a student under Hall at Johns Hopkins in 1886.

[d]Only three people besides myself have ever actually studied Hall's manuscript dissertation (Hall 1878a)—Dorothy Ross, Ignas Skrupskelis, and Thomas Cadwallader.

[e]Harvard lists Hall's dissertation as "The Perception of Space," published in modified form under the title "The Muscular Perception of Space," in Hall (1868b).

moral philosophy, but a work that might conceivably pass as a statement on the then-modern philosophy of science.

Note, for instance, Hall's final paragraph:

Even so far as it is a matter of belief we prefer to plight our allegiance to a programme of work yet to be done though it were far more indefinite than it is rather than to face a blank wall of nescience whereon no other record can be read than that where the individual limits of development or culture were mistakenly and arrogantly asserted to be the limits of possible knowledge. Psychology is no longer content to hold belief in an external world as a mere act of faith or opinion. She postulates an ultimate monism, and hopes one day to prove a rightful title to the bold nomenclature of the identity-philosophy. Now with true Socratic irony she dares to take for the most part the attitude of ignorance toward an absolute-philosophy and yet more absolute science. Whether she disclose a messianic function, and gladden the long travail of thought by never dispensing the transcendent secret of reason incarnate in organic life, the future alone will tell. (Hall 1878c, 43–44)

This grandiloquent finale is immediately followed by a note in the hand of William James, which reads: "Disclaiming any responsibility for the doctrines and arguments herein contained, this Thesis is approved as affording sufficient evidence of original thought and research to make the writer a fit candidate for the Ph.D."

Secondly, nowhere does Bowditch's signature appear on the dissertation. The signatures were Francis Bowen, William James, and Frederick Henry Hedge. Bowen was the senior member of the Philosophy Department at the time, an ardent Unitarian and defender of Agassiz's creationist theories of evolution; James was still an assistant professor of philosophy, teaching the new physiological psychology, but also dealing in Spencer and the British empiricists; and Hedge, a member of Emerson's transcendentalist circle, schooled in the German rationalist interpretation of Biblical texts, was Professor of German and Instructor in Ecclesiastical History. Bowditch does not officially enter into Hall's credentialing process, except that we do know he was present at Hall's oral thesis defense.*ᶠ* Rather, Bowditch's influence must be reconstructed along more indirect lines. But for the time being, suffice it to say that Hall came to Harvard to study the new science and received instruction from James in psychology and from Bowditch in physiology. He availed himself of every opportunity to become part of the new science, but remained to the end of this phase of his career ever immersed in a distorted

---

*ᶠ*The oral defense was conducted by James, Bowditch, Everett, Hedge, and Palmer in June 1878 (Ross 1972, 79).

hybrid of moral philosophy and German idealism that was of his own making.

HALL'S EARLY CAREER

Upon graduation, Hall's prospects for a position in either philosophy or psychology in the United States were practically nil. He had vainly applied to the newly founded Johns Hopkins University, but its President, Daniel Coit Gilman, was already making tentative offers to James. Hall may have harbored secret hopes that James would accept so that Hall himself might be considered to fill the Harvard vacancy, but fate and time were against him. With some savings, an unexpected gift, and much encouragement from others, Hall, having been much stimulated by an earlier trip abroad before his stint at Harvard, decided to return to Germany for further study. He sailed in the late summer of 1878. His plan was to study physics and physiology in Berlin with Helmholtz and DuBois Reymond, and then to proceed to Leipzig to take up physiology and psychology under Ludwig and Wundt. He was entranced with Helmholtz's agenda to express the phenomena of consciousness in terms of chemistry and physics. In Leipzig, Hall's association with Bowditch gave him entré to Ludwig's laboratory, and he became the first American student of psychology to study experimental laboratory methods under Wundt's guidance. As his own mastery of the literature and expertise in the laboratory became more exact, Hall even came to denigrate Wundt for his vagueness. Eventually, he would return to America as a fearless exponent of the new scientific German approach to psychology. But before he made this commitment, Hall continued to waver upon his choice of vocation, still torn between medicine and philosophy.

In the fall of 1878, Hall corresponded with both James and Bowditch, reporting on his studies in Germany. To Bowditch he communicated the latest developments in physiology and aided in the procurement of apparatus. To James, he reported as well on the state of both psychology and psychiatry. His biographer, Dorothy Ross, makes a special point to note that in Germany Hall had the study of psychopathology open to him, an avenue which had been denied him at Harvard, although Hall's interest had been piqued by James's involvement in the field (Ross 1972, 83).

The somatic bias in Germany psychiatry supported Hall's physicalist views. He was impressed by the post-mortem examinations done at the Charité Clinic in Berlin, and he developed an acquaintance with Paul Flechsig, his neighbor, and a new professor of psychiatry at Leipzig (Ross 1972, 83). Hall gained clinical contact with mental illness through his frequent contacts with Karl Westphal, Professor of Psychiatry at the University of Berlin and medical director of the Charité. Hall's ward visits and discussions with Westphal were duly reported to William James (p. 84). Later in 1879, Hall inspected psychiatric facilities in Italy and Austria, and he made a report to James, expressing great shock at the condition of Italian asylums. He heard Meynert lecture on psychiatry in Vienna and toured his hospital. Hall briefly observed Charcot's demonstrations of hypnosis in Paris and Bernheim's in Nancy. Thus Ross concludes, "[Hall's] . . . subjective and scientific interest in mental illness, supported by clinical experience in Europe, would later develop into one of the principal bases of his psychology." (p. 84)

Also during this time, Hall's conception of himself in relation to James began to change. At first, Hall expressed his gratitude to James repeatedly in numerous letters, even proclaiming himself James's disciple and best advocate (Ross 1972, 81, 86). James wrote that he intended to come to Europe in 1880 and would talk with Hall there. But Hall wrote back warning his old teacher how much more of an empiricist he had become, thinking James would find him no longer congenial. They met in Heidelberg in July, attended lectures, and walked through the hills outside the town, talking incessantly. James reported to Bowditch that their conversations ran nearly unabated for three 12- to 13-hour periods (p. 87). After this episode, James proclaimed that Hall had advanced so much that their student-master roles had become reversed.

Hall no doubt took him literally, for he at once gathered up his nerve and cast his net into James's own waters. He would write his own textbook of psychology. But his first cast, like many to follow, was a failure. By this time, Hall had conceived of a comprehensive psychology built up on mechanistic principles of reflex action. He corresponded with James about the project and opened negotiations with Henry Holt for publication a little after Holt had contracted with James to write a similar text in psychology. But Hall's project came to nothing, while James's did appear, albeit ten years late.

In another episode about this same time, James even roused Hall's ire. In "The Sentiment of Rationality," James developed a major statement on his pluralistic view by articulating arguments against the evolutionary monism of "Clifford, Taine, Spencer, Fechner, Zöllner, G. S. Hall, and others" (Ross 1972, 77). Even though Hall had proclaimed such a monistic position in his thesis, he vigorously objected to James in a letter dated October 1879, saying: "Would you mind omitting my name from the list of hylozoic atomists? No doubt you are perfectly justified from your letters and my 'Space,' but I *meant* only monism, as a postulate, or scientific hypothesis, and by no means as a proven truth" (pp. 91–92). Even after this, their exchanges remained amicable, but an increasing polarization became apparent.

In the fall of 1879, Hall surprised everyone with news that he had married in Berlin. His wife was Cornelia Fisher, a young woman whom he had met in Yellow Springs, Ohio, and who was now studying art abroad.

Even as James noted a new strength and confidence in his friend's subsequent letters, their growing estrangement was underscored when Hall's marriage was made known only through a postscript in a letter to Bowditch, a slight that cannot have failed to cause James some degree of chagrin.

Poor and unknown, Hall and his new bride returned to America in early 1880 with no prospects. He settled the two of them in a little apartment in Somerville, within walking distance of Harvard and Cambridge. He re-associated himself informally with James and Bowditch, paddled around in Bowditch's laboratory doing experiments (Bowditch and Hall 1882), and kept a keen eye out for openings anywhere, especially at Johns Hopkins and at Harvard, but none appeared.

There were several attempts made on Hall's behalf, however. James had declined Gilman's offer to lecture at Johns Hopkins for two or three months in 1879, putting Hall forward as the more appropriate candidate, but to no avail. James tried even more forcefully in 1880, but again Hall was rebuffed by Gilman. Hall, meanwhile, still coveted a professorship at Harvard. James might go to Hopkins or one of the older professors might retire. Hall had applied for the Plummer Professorship of Christian Morals in early 1881, hoping that his physiological bias would not hurt him. He was reluctant to preach, however, and was dead set against doing any pastoral work with students. James noted that Hall's critique of philosophy in American universities had been poorly received at Harvard, and although Hall thought the reaction unjust, Ross notes that he later regretted writing the piece. As recompense, James tried to secure Hall a Lowell lectureship, but in this he also failed (Ross 1972, 105 fn).

During his second trip abroad, Ross notes that, despondent about the poor prospects of making a living at physiology and philosophy, Hall began to think seriously again about studying medicine. But he then decided on the application of psychology to education as a more promising alternative (Ross 1972, 106). As if it were an afterthought, in order to cover as many bases as possible, Hall had made a frantic tour of schools in Germany, France, and England in his last months before returning to America. Within a year, he would publish his first papers on pedagogy and the mental life of the child. This is as much as his biographer says about the origins of Hall's interest in a field in which he would soon become a recognized leader.[g]

As it turned out, President Eliot invited Hall to give a series of lectures on pedagogy at Harvard during 1881. After their delivery in Cambridge, Gilman offered Hall a similar series at Johns Hopkins, where Hall delivered ten lectures on psychology in January, 1882 (Ross 1972, 134–135). In March 1882, Hall was finally offered a three-year appointment in the phil-

---

[g]For more on Hall's contribution to this field, see Siegel and White 1981 and White 1988.

osophy department at Johns Hopkins as lecturer in psychology and pedagogy, where he joined George S. Morris, his old friend, and C. S. Peirce, whom he had come to admire. All three were part-timers until Gilman could find a full professor to replace them. Peirce was dismissed in 1884, however, and Gilman, having to choose between Morris and Hall, offered Hall the full professorship. James had previously made a strong suggestion that Hall might be a link between the University and the pending medical school, and, in addition to Hall's other qualities, this likely appealed to Gilman. It was under this set of circumstances that Hall ascended to the professorship at Johns Hopkins (pp. 136–137).

But Hall was by no means finished with James and Bowditch, even though he appeared to have found a niche at Hopkins and was at least in some way launched in the new science. While he continued to regard Bowditch as a venerated mentor, he still attempted to draw him into various schemes.

In one instance, Hall tried to gain credentials as a physician. James, as we have said, had originally recommended Hall to Gilman as a potential link between the University and the new medical school, which was still in the planning stage. Hall, however, always the opportunist, did not wait for the formal inauguration of a medical school. Once he had begun his teaching duties, he opened his courses particularly to those interested in psychiatric medicine. He included lectures on the psychological aspects of insanity and he took his students regularly to Bay View, the local institution for the pauper insane, a facility that was a part of the city's almshouse and was filled with the incurable, the unmanageable, the penniless, and the dying.[b]

In early 1886, it appeared that Bay View would be tied into the new medical school at Hopkins, and three doctors were appointed as visiting physicians. Hall was appointed to cooperate with them "as an expert in the management of insane asylums" (Ross 1972, 160). To what extent he was actually the superintendent is not clear, for he would have been the only non-M.D. in the United States to run an asylum.

Likely anticipating these events, in April 1885 Hall had written to Bowditch with an inquiry. As his tastes and interests were drawing him more to making psychiatry the theoretical focus of his psychology, he wondered whether Harvard would consider granting him an honorary M.D. Hall further explained that his purpose was not to enter into medical practice, but only to procure further psychological and educational opportunities (Ross 1972, 159). We do not know the substance of Bowditch's reply, but it is a known fact that Hall never received that honor from Harvard or anywhere else.

[b]Ross also notes that one of Hall's first fellows was William Noyes, Jr., a graduate of Harvard Medical School, intern at the Danvers State Hospital in Massachusetts, and a former colleague in Bowditch's laboratory (Ross 1972, 159).

There is a footnote to add to this story. It is probably only a typographical error, or the mistaken, foregone conclusion of some anonymous assistant typing final copy. In 1887, the International Medical Congress held its meetings in Washington D.C. and in their *Transactions,* one can read in the opening section on Psychological Medicine and Nervous Diseases, under the listing of Officers, that on the council was a "G. Stanley Hall, A.M., M.D." (Hamilton 1887, 225).

HALL'S STUDY OF HYPNOSIS

There occurred yet another incident while Hall was at Johns Hopkins, which served to separate him even further from James. In the early 1880s, among other topics in philosophy and psychology, Hall had published a review of German studies on hypnosis, and then presented the results of experiments he had performed upon his return. This further work, Hall said, was a continuation of his work with Bowditch and was based on his frequent association with one of James's New York colleagues, George Miller Beard.[i]

Hall's investigation of hypnosis in Bowditch's laboratory was not published until 1883, after Hall was established at Johns Hopkins. His study, supporting the concentration theory of the trance state, allied Hall with the tradition that claimed the nonpathological character of the phenomenon. His hypothesis was that intensified attention reduces reaction time. Hall's study, "Reaction Time and Attention in the Hypnotic State," used as the sole subject A. B., a 30-year-old cabinetmaker who was prone to sleepwalking from boyhood.

Most tests which had been administered by skeptical physicians on A.B. to determine the authenticity of his abnormal state had been of the extreme variety—pistols discharged near the ear, sharp instruments thrust into his body, caustic substances applied to such sensitive body parts as his nose and mouth and nostrils, and strong electric shocks given through various parts of his torso. Hall reported that the subject was hence naturally disinclined to participate in any more experiments, and it was only with difficulty that he induced the man to visit the laboratory. A friend had to accompany the subject, Hall had to abstain from anything painful or unpleasant, and some small pecuniary compensation was also arranged.

Hall based his theoretical approach on Braid's description of hypnosis as

[i]Ross 1972, 148–150. Ross notes that Hall had developed a simple mechanistic model of psychophysiological processes that would allow him to find the elementary unity of consciousness bridging mind and the material world. He thought his study of optical illusions in Bowditch's laboratory had brought him, "very near attaining the quale of a real, pure sensation." His study of hypnotism, however, later led him to a more sophisticated view of mental function.

a study in the pathology of attention. Heidenhain in Germany had made important experiments in this direction, but he had stopped experimenting when Burger showed that all his effects might be produced by suggestion. Hall noted that it was George Miller Beard in New York who had most persistently urged this explanation beginning in 1877.

Hall countered this view with the opinion that in nearly all the recent studies of reaction time, the most effective way the subject might reduce the time was by a strong concentration of attention upon the expected stimulus and the intended reaction. Hall's real intention was to submit the hypnotic subject to the prevailing physiological theory of attention put forth by Wundt, who thought that, although fatigue, practice, and strength of the stimulus were cofactors, reaction time might be diminished by "opening certain nerve-tracts or by preparatory innervation of the reacting muscles."

Hall began first by a comparison of reaction times in the normal and hypnotic state. He ran the subject through a series of reaction-time measurements, gave him a few minutes' rest, and then had the subject mesmerized. Most subjects in the normal state were unable to keep their attention on the reaction-time apparatus for very long, but this subject, while hypnotized, proved easily able to do so. In fact, Hall noted that the subject began pressing the reaction key with increasing vigor until near the end of the session, when his movements became violent, prolonged, and almost cramped, although these efforts did not speed up his reaction time at all. A total of three observations were made over a period of three weeks. Comparing the averages, Hall found reaction time in the hypnotic condition to be slightly better than in the normal state, but had to admit the results were actually inconclusive.

Along with these observations, Hall also performed a series of simple association-time studies on A.B. and another subject after the method of Galton and Wundt. Lists of familiar words were given to the hypnotized subject and his reaction time as well as the response word he gave were noted. A.B. was asked to respond to 40 words in the normal state, then three days later the same 40 words in the hypnotized condition, and so on, until he had responded to a total of 360. Hall stated that the reaction time was shorter in the hypnotized condition, but the numerical data were not presented.

One of four pieces that William James claimed as his only contribution to the experimental literature was a replication of Hall's study, published in the *Proceedings of the American Society for Psychical Research* (James 1887a). James tested the same theory that Hall had put forward by collecting data from 806 trials on three different subjects, all Harvard seniors, using reaction-time equipment and a Baltzar's kymograph. Hall had stated that his data showed that reaction time was faster during trance than when the subject was measured both before and after. By a comparison of simple mathematical averages, James showed, however, that in his own subjects the trance actually slowed reaction time, which only slightly improved once the trance had ended. Rather than presuming he had established anything definite, James merely concluded that Hall's assertion was by no means proven. He implied that Hall's subject may have been acting out the subconscious desires of the experimenter; and that at the very least, one "should beware of making rash generalizations from few cases about the hypnotic state."

James thus criticized Hall for his poor methodology, reproving him twice, once for his inchoate experimental practices and again for his attempt to penetrate into the field of hypnotism, which was a decidedly French enterprise and weakly treated in German science.

HALL VERSUS JAMES ON PSYCHOLOGY

Hall seems to have saved his venom for the pages of the *American Journal of Psychology*, which he had then recently launched, and which would become an instrument of ideological revenge against all his detractors. James had good-naturedly called it something of a confidence game, because Hall had collected subscriptions more than a year before it first appeared. In one letter, James compared Hall's forthcoming publication to his own journal, the *Proceedings of the American Society for Psychical Research*. James had produced this publication between 1885 and 1889, and referred to it as a competitive standard that Hall might like to use to strengthen his own new venture.[j] It is also a fact that Hall never asked James to submit a paper to the *American Journal of Psychology*, although James tried to offer him something in the beginning.[k] James, in fact, never did publish in the pages of Hall's journal.

As well, the two of them remained divided over psychical research. Both James and Hall had been founding Vice Presidents of the American Society for Psychical Research in 1884. but memberships on all the research committees fell into the hands of Harvard scientists and philosophers, making it difficult to have meetings in New York, Philadelphia, or Washington. Hall was excluded by distance and dropped out after a few years. Finally, in the

[j]I do hope and trust you'll publish it on date like mine, or else not date the numbers like Pflüger's *Archiv* . . . " (James 1886)

[k]"Had you given me earlier notice of your intentions, I could have sent you an article on 'The Perception of Time,' which is now in Harris's hands for his *so genannten* 'October' number of last year. I am very sorry for the mischance. I didn't think much of it, but Harris welcomes it as a 'superb contribution to the new Psychology,' whatever that may be. I am able to send you a few little empirical scraps within the year, though I am doing now no experimental work" (James to Hall 1887c).

opening issue of the *American Journal of Psychology,* Hall went to great lengths to distance himself from the psychical researchers with a scathing critique of their methods, particularly the English circle grouped around James's friends, Myers, Podmore, and Gurney.

James replied that "to take sides as positively as you do now and on general philosophical grounds, seems to me a very dangerous and unscientific attitude." Characterizing the two of them, James said: "I should express the difference between our two positions in the matter, by calling mine a baldly empirical one, and yours, one due to a general theoretic creed. . . . I don't think it exactly fair to make the issue what you make it—one between Science and Superstition" (James to Hall 1887b).

Similarly, Hall began his journal by calling the entire field of the New Psychology physiological, but he quickly shifted to more subtle descriptive categories. "Experimental psychology" meant German experimental laboratory psychophysics, while "psychopathology," referred to the French studies on hysteria and hypnosis. This distinction was meant to carry the implication that psychopathology, and anything connected with it, especially psychical research, was something less than scientific in the eyes of the Germans, as well as Hall, himself.

James, for his part, seems to have held no rancor. When his monumental *Principles of Psychology* came out in 1890, he lauded Hall in the preface for the many hours, they had shared in conversation about important psychological problems. In the body of the text, James claimed he stood for a positivistic psychology free of metaphysics, a position which he cleaved to, more or less, as he tried to negotiate a discussion on various aspects of the scientific study of consciousness. Hall responded in his review of the book by calling James a mere *"impressionist* in psychology." Later, when Hall published a history of the founders of modern psychology, as if to write him out of the annals of psychology's scientific origins, James was not mentioned in it.

One must understand that by 1891, both Hall's personal and professional life were seemingly coming undone. At home, the previous spring, he had lost his wife and daughter, who were found accidently asphyxiated. At work, in the second year of Hall's presidency of the newly opened Clark University, President William Rainey Harper of the University of Chicago had swooped down and raided Hall's school of its best faculty. The worst of it, however, was that during this same period Jonas Clark, the University's chief financial backer, had begun to lose interest in Hall's venture. Hall was by then a man in desperate straits.

Thus, it is plausible to suggest that by 1892, Hall was motivated to convene the first meeting of the American Psychological Association in order to retrieve lost ground. What he needed was a way to regain national stature, for Clark, for psychology, and for himself. Scholars are in doubt however, as to exactly who was actually present at the first meeting, which was held on 8 July 1892. Fernberger (1943) reported that, in addition to Hall, George Fullerton, William James, Joseph Jastrow, George T. Ladd, James McKeen Cattell, and James Mark Baldwin were present. But after interviewing Cattell and Jastrow, who were still alive in the 1940s, Fernberger found that they were absent, along with at least James. Hall was obviously the convener, but additional scholarly research will have to tell who was actually there. Hopefully, we will find that Hall did not have to convene the meeting solely by himself.

JAMES'S PRESIDENTIAL ADDRESS TO THE APA

Hall was president the first year, Ladd the second. An official constitution was not adopted until 1894, and in that year William James was elected president. His acceptance address was important because it announced to psychologists the need to correct a basic misinterpretation that was rapidly gaining currency as the accepted definition of scientific psychology. It was also the first time that James articulated to so large and important an audience of psychologists the basic idea that later came to be known as his metaphysic of radical empiricism.

Originally delivered as "The Knowing of Things Together," and published under the alternative title "The Tigers in India," James used the occasion of his presidential address to the professional psychologists of the United States as the platform to state openly the unequivocal dependence of science on metaphysics, a position he had earlier denied in the *Principles* (James 1895a).

James began by taking up the question of the synthetic unity of consciousness. "Knowing" is the first problem, defining "things" another, and accounting for the experience of their unity yet another.

In the first case, James presented his well-known distinction between knowledge about versus acquaintance with. Knowing about is representative knowledge. "The Tigers in India," James said, calls forth an image in our minds without our having any direct contact with the reality of the relevant phenomena. While it is true that we must have some direct experience at some point in some way with tigers and with India in order to know the meaning of the two ideas together, we certainly do not need to directly confront a tiger in India to know the words' referent. Nevertheless, we know that the phrase does refer to some reality in human experience.

Acquaintance with, on the other hand, is direct knowledge, immediately experienced and intuitively known. There is no presence in absence, no pointing to something else, only the bare relation between my consciousness and the thing as directly apprehended in itself. Standing in India, there is only myself and the tiger.

What lies at the intersection of these two ways of knowing is James's struggle. There is immediate experience and our categories about it, both of which must converge in the present moment. But the present moment he points out is a convenient fiction, since nothing remains stable. Thus we can speak only of the passing moment as the only thing that ever concretely was or is or shall be. In the ever-changing present, there is a sense of the past and a portent of the future. Within this minimal pulse of experience, we must find an explanation for how we experience things as a unity.

James's strategy was then somewhat tentative. He provided no final answer, but rather reviewed the various explanations that had been put forth to account for the unity of experience—physiological, psychological, animistic, and transcendental. In this vein, he spent the greater part of his speech discussing theories of attention, reminiscence, synergy, the individual soul, the World Soul, and how we relate to the self and to other objects.

He then said:

You will agree with me that I have brought no new insight to the subject, and that I have only gossiped to while away this unlucky presidential hour to which the constellations doomed me at my birth. But since gossip we have had to have, let me make the hour more gossipy still by saying a final word about the position taken up in my own *Principles of Psychology*. . . . (James 1895a, 86)

He wanted to take up the subject, he said, because in 1890 he had stated that in order that psychology be considered a natural science, it should clearly abandon all attempts to ascertain how we come to know things together. States of consciousness, which depend on brain states, are the only vehicle of knowledge we need to suppose. Now, by 1894, he had undergone a complete change of mind. Thus, he announced

My intention was a good one, and a natural science infinitely more complete than the psychologies we now possess could be written without abandoning its terms. Like all authors, I have, therefore, been surprised that this child of my genius should not be more admired by others— should, in fact, have been generally either misunderstood or despised. But do not fear that on this occasion I am either going to defend or to re-explain the bantling. I am going to make things more harmonious by simply giving it up. (James 1895a, 88)

He proceeded to explain that since publishing his book he had reached the conclusion, "that no conventional restrictions *can* keep metaphysical and so-called epistemological inquiries out of the psychology-books." The chief

reasons he gave were based on his study of the broad field then called psychopathology:

> I see, moreover, better now than then, that my proposal to designate mental states merely by their cognitive function leads to a somewhat strained way of talking about dreams and reveries, and to quite an unnatural way of talking of some emotional states.

He then stated a correction:

> I am willing, consequently, henceforward, that mental contents should be called complex, just as their objects are, and this even in psychology. Not because their parts are separable, as parts of objects are; not because they have an eternal or quasi-eternal individual existence, like the parts of objects; for the various "fields" of which they are parts are integers, existentially, and their parts only live as long as *they* live. Still, *in* them, we can call parts, parts.—But when, without circumlocution or disguise, I thus come over to your views, I insist that those of you who applaud me (if any such there be) should recognize the obligations which the new agreement imposes on yourselves. Not till you have dropped the old phrases, so absurd or so empty, . . . not till you have in your turn suc-ceeded in some such long inquiry into conditions as the one I have just failed in; not till you have laid bare more of the nature of that altogether unique kind of complexity in unity which mental states involve; not till then, I say, will psychology reach any real benefit from the conciliatory spirit of which I have done what I can to set an example. (James 1895a, 88–89)

In other words, if there is no science free of metaphysics, then the compromise must be to acknowledge that empirical research is more com-plex than a simplistic subject-object dichotomy would presuppose. The complexity of mental states means that it is to the phenomenology of the science-making process itself that we must look to see the metaphysics at work (Taylor 1992). Scientists have, in fact, an obligation to acknowledge this state of affairs if research is to go on. Only then, James felt, can psychol-ogy evolve into a first-rate science.

CONTROVERSY OVER THE FIRST LABORATORY

One cannot underestimate how extraordinarily influential James was in American psychology at that time. Until the day that he died, and even after, he remained a symbol to so many of Americanism, individuality, freedom, and open-mindedness. He had his great supporters in such figures as Ladd, Baldwin, Royce, Dewey, and Angell. Nevertheless, particularly within scientific psychology as a burgeoning profession, James also had his detractors. The most forceful group, who were not necessarily anti-Jamesean so much as supporters of an experimentalism in psychology that James did not agree with, were the various waves of American students returning mainly from Leipzig with doctorates in the new science. All were eager to get on with the business of building a new profession, which they accomplished not only by launching the APA, but also through the establishment of experimental laboratories at colleges and universities throughout the United States. Hall and Cattell were among the first wave, followed by Münsterberg, whom James brought to Harvard, and Titchener, an Englishman who aspired to become the American Wundt and who settled at Cornell. Then there was Lightner Witmer, Frank Angell, and others.

To Americans, James was the preeminent psychologist. This meant that what he represented, namely, the study of consciousness, the mind-body problem, abnormal psychology, psychical research, and the philosophical foundations of science, to a large degree constituted the public perception of what the new psychology was all about. The new scientific psychologists returning from Germany seemed forced at every turn to justify their new definition of experimental psychology as more scientific by contrasting it against the Jamesean view.

A case in point is the claim that Hall made in 1895 in his journal that *he* had founded the first laboratory in the United States devoted to experimental psychology, instancing the laboratory he created at Johns Hopkins in 1885. In the same breath, he also claimed that subsequently his various students at Johns Hopkins went off after graduation to found all the other laboratories in the Unite States, including the laboratory at Harvard.

Immediately, a great hue and cry went up from several quarters, and James McKeen Cattell, as editor of *Science*, main organ of the Association for the Advancement of Science, found himself at the center of an exchange between G. Stanley Hall, William James, James Mark Baldwin, and others.

James's letter is dated 19 October 1895 from the Psychological Laboratory, Harvard University:

To the Editor of *Science: The American Journal of Psychology* began a new series last week with an "editorial" introduction, in which some most extraordinary statements appear. As an official of Harvard University I cannot let one of these pass without public contradiction. The editorial says (on the top of page 4) that the "department of experimental psychology and laboratory" at Harvard was "founded under the influence" of some unspecified person mentioned in a list of President Hall's pupils. I, myself "founded" the instruction in experimental psychology at Harvard in 1874–75, or 1876, I forget which. For a long series of years the laboratory was in two rooms of the Scientific School building, which at last became choked with apparatus, so that a change was necessary. I then, in 1890, resolved on an altogether new departure, raised several thousand dollars, fitted up Dane Hall, and introduced laboratory exercises as a regular part of the undergraduate psychology course. Dr. Herbert Nichols, than at Clark, was appointed, in 1891, assistant in this part of the work; and when Professor Münsterberg was made director of the laboratory, in 1892, and I went for a year to Europe, Dr. Nichols gave my undergraduate course. I owe him my heartiest thanks for his services and "influence" in the graduate as well as the undergraduate department at Harvard, but I imagine him to have been as much surprised as myself at the statement in the editorial from which I quote—a statement the more remarkable in that the chief editor of the American Journal studied experimental psychology himself at Harvard from 1877 to 1879. (James 1895b)

Besides this published statement, James also wrote Hall a personal letter expressing his reservations:

I have just received No. 1, of your new series of the A. J. of P. and no one can be gladder than I of the improvements that it promises or wish it more permanent prosperity. I am astonished however to find you asserting that the department of exp. psych. and the lab. at Harvard was founded under the influence of a Clark man. The only Clark man possible was Nichols who came after the lab. was founded. *You will of course rectify this error in your next number.* Another extraordinary bit of mistatement of fact is that the function of the publishing investigations in psychophysics laboratories is not yet represented by any serial publication in English. Have you ever opened the Psychological Review? I think you owe *it* also an apology in your next number.

As an arm-chair professor, I frankly admit my general inferiority as a laboratory-teacher and investigator. But some little regard should be paid to the good will with which I have tried to force my nature, and to the actual things I have done. One of them for example was in directing you in experimental investigation, with very naive methods, it is true, but you may remember that there was no other place but Harvard where during those years you could get even that. I also remember giving a short course of psychological lectures at the Johns Hopkins years before you went there. They were exclusively experimental and I have been told, made an "epoch" there in determining opinion.

I will recognize how contemptible these beginnings were, and that you and your pupils have in these latter years left them far behind. But you are now professing to state history, beginnings are a part thereof, and should not be written down in inverted order. The statement that experimental psychology at Harvard came from Clark is simply ridiculous. In this world we all owe [some debt] to each other. My debt to you and to Clark is great, and if only my own person was concerned, I should let you say what you like and not object, for the bystanders generally see truly. In this case, however, the mistake must concern the credit of my university, so I must insist on a correction in your next issue. (James 1895c)

I shall confine myself only to a few major points brought out by James's response. One is that James never laid any claim to being the first to found a laboratory, and it was only when driven to the wall by the absurdity of Hall's assertion that he felt compelled to state his view of the matter for the record. It seems clear enough that in Hall's mind, James was not to be considered an experimental scientist and that the Harvard laboratory was never official until 1891, when Nichols came in anticipation of Münsterberg's arrival a year later. James, on the other hand, saw his lab in the 1870s as an entirely legitimate enterprise that deserved recognition, and he saw himself as teaching Hall experimental psychology at the time.

Another point is that, despite loud testimonials to the contrary by James, Baldwin, and others in the pages of *Science*, it is surprising the number of historians and psychologists who continue to believe Hall's version to this day. When inaugurating the newly founded experimental laboratory at Wittenberg College in 1917, Cattell, himself, gave Hall credit for founding the first laboratory in America. Gardner Murphy's *Historical Introduction to Modern Psychology* (1929) states the same, and in 1985, Johns Hopkins erroneously celebrated the centennial of the "founding" of its psychological laboratory by Hall one hundred years earlier, with a symposium of papers subsequently published as a book (Cattell 1928; Murphy 1949, 168; Hulse and Green 1986).

Finally, it should come as no surprise that Hall, of course, never printed any kind of correction.

The following fifteen years of the relationship between William James and G. Stanley Hall might be described as one of measured détente. Hall for his part was miffed that Harvard was building an experimental department around Münsterberg that would rival his own efforts in graduate psychology at Clark. Harvard, meanwhile, tried simply to ignore what was going on out in Worcester. Robert Mearns Yerkes, on first arriving in Cambridge in 1897, has described his impressions of the situation:

> All the while I knew of lively interest in comparative psychology at Clark University, but I was given to understand that it was either indiscreet or bad form for a Harvard psychologist to try to cultivate friendly professional relations with G. Stanley Hall and his Clark associates. (Yerkes 1943, 75)

Meanwhile, following Janet's work in Paris, William James and his colleagues Morton Prince and James Jackson Putnam had launched the so-called Boston School of Abnormal Psychology after 1896 (Taylor 1982). James began teaching a graduate course in mental pathology in 1893, Putnam experimented with psychotherapy in the context of neurology, and Prince began his pioneering studies of multiple personality. Their collective activities at Harvard, the Massachusetts General Hospital, and the Boston City Hospital made Boston the center of developments in scientific psychotherapy in the English-speaking world.

At the same time, Hall, not to be outdone, conspired with Edward Cowles at the McLean Asylum to bring Adolf Meyer to Worcester, so that Meyer could teach psychopathology at Clark. Following up on this line, Hall then invited the distinguished neuropathologist, August Forel, Meyers's teacher from Zurich who was the former head of the Burghölzli Asylum, to deliver the decennial lecture in 1899 honoring the founding of Clark University. Forel lectured on an important topic related to the mind-body problem, hypnotism and cerebral activity, which undoubtedly caught the attention of the Boston psychotherapists.

Within a few years, major developments in scientific psychotherapy would take place in Boston. Medical and psychiatric social service would be founded at the Massachusetts General Hospital. Group psychotherapy would begin with tuberculosis patients, and clinical trials to test the various psychotherapeutic methods were initiated (Taylor 1988). In 1906 alone, Morton Prince launched the *Journal of Abnormal Psychology* and published his famous *Dissociation of a personality*; Cabot, Putnam, Coriat, and Worcester launched the Emmanuel Movement, an experiment in Christian psychotherapy that would later become the basis for clinical pastoral education in America; Janet delivered his triumphant lectures to national acclaim on the major symptoms of hysteria in order to inaugurate the opening of the new Harvard Medical School quadrangle; and William James presented his Lowell lectures on pragmatism, the philosophical ethic of an America era. There can be little doubt that, in the aftermath of these developments, Hall began to conspire a year or two later to shift the psychotherapeutic spotlight out to Worcester. His plan eventually led to the now famous conference of 1909, when Freud and Jung came to speak at Clark (Taylor 1985).

CONCLUSION

We have gone far beyond the founding of the APA in 1892. But by so doing, we have seen that the encounter between Hall and James produced some of the great skirmishes in the early history of scientific psychology in America. Suffice it to say here that Hall's star only began its ascent in the 1880s. As Ross notes, between 1880 and 1890, Hall's reputation as a psychologist in America had risen so much that in prominence he was second only to William James, (although we are certain that Hall must have thought of himself as first) (Ross 1972, 103).

Ross has characterized Hall's relationship with James as a passionate acquiescence, with an underlying fear and propitiatory retreat. Hall treated James with an ambivalent attachment, as he did William T. Harris and George Morris. Nevertheless, Hall and James were similar in several ways. They were only two years apart in age. Both had adolescent crises that extended into adulthood. Both married late. Both held similar views on the relation of the nervous system to education. Both retained an interest in religious experience and embodied the older tradition of moral philosophy in their ideas about consciousness, while at the same time both worked as pioneers in establishing psychology as a science.

Yet both differed in their definition of what was legitimately to be called experimental psychology. Hall came to the new psychology through Hegel and Wundt, James through the American pragmatist movement, British Empiricism, and the French experimental tradition in physiology. While Hall is remembered as an exponent of German laboratory science, father of the child study movement, and educator, there is ample evidence that in his heart of hearts he really wanted to be a physician, a desire partly inspired by William James. But philosophically he was repelled by what he saw as the loose nature of James's thinking, and in the mature phase of his professional life, everywhere he had the opportunity, either by accident or design, Hall seemed to write James out of the history of the discipline.

James, for his part, well-to-do Harvard professor who could afford to speak his mind and who certainly was not confronted by the daunting obstacles that Hall faced establishing himself, gave rightful credit where it was due, but took no umbrage with Hall, a farm-boy-turned-intellectual, when it came to stating the essential epistemological issues confronting psychology at the time.

That there is no purely objective science free from of metaphysics; that positivistic science is itself based upon an implied metaphysics of physical-ism; and that psychology is uniquely positioned of all the sciences to fathom the phenomenology of the science-making process as a method of self-renovation, are all Jamesean ideas that are still alive and well in the current debates over the present status and future direction of the discipline.

Could the force and direction of these arguments, already suffusing the relation between Hall and James in 1892, been a factor in the events that surrounded the founding and early history of the American Psychological Association? The presumption is strongly in the affirmative.

REFERENCES

BEHRENS, P. J. 1986. The centennial of America's first doctorate in psychology: J. Jastrow. Paper presented at the Eighteenth annual meeting of Cheiron, Inter-national Society for History of the Behavioral and Social Sciences, University of Guelph, June 11, 1986.

BOSTON SOCIETY OF MEDICAL SCIENCES. 1877. Minutes. On deposit, Harvard Medi-cal Archives. Countway Library of Medicine. Boston.

BOWDITCH, H. P. & G. S. HALL. 1882. Optical illusions of motion. J. Physiol. **3:** 297–307.

CATTELL, J. M. 1928. Early psychological laboratories. Science **67:** 543–548.

FERNBERGER, S. W. 1943. The American Psychological Association, 1892–1942. Psychol. Rev. **50:** 33–60.

HALL, G. S. 1878a. Dissertation Register accompanying "The perception of space." Harvard Archives. Pusey Library. Cambridge, MA.

HALL, G. S. 1878b. The muscular perception of space. Mind **3:** 433–450.

HALL, G. S. 1878c. The Perception of Space (Ph.D. dissertation). Pusey Library, H.U. 90.220. Harvard University. Cambridge, MA.

HALL, G. S. 1879. Laura Bridgman. Mind **4:** 149–172.

HAMILTON, J. B., Ed. 1887. Transactions of the International Medical Congress. Ninth session. Vol. 5, p. 225. Washington, DC.

HARPER, R. S. 1949. Tables of American doctorates in psychology. Am. J. Psychol. **62:** 579–587.

HULSE, S. H. & B. GREEN, JR., Eds. 1986. One Hundred Years of Psychological Research in America: G. Stanley Hall and the Johns Hopkins Tradition. Johns Hopkins University Press. Baltimore, MD.

JAMES, W. 1876. The teaching of philosophy in our colleges. The Nation Sept. 21, 1876: 178–179.

JAMES, W. 1878. Brute and human intellect. J. Specul. Philos. **12:** 236–276.

JAMES, W. 1882. On some Hegelisms. Mind **7:** 186–208.

JAMES, W. 1886, to G. S. Hall, Tamworth Iron Works, New Hampshire, Aug. 1. Hall Papers, Clark University Archives. Worcester, MA. By permission.

JAMES, W. 1887a. Reaction-time in the hypnotic trance. Proc. Am. Soc. Psychical Res. **1:** 246–248.

JAMES, W. 1887b, to G. S. Hall, 18 Garden St., Cambridge, MA, November 5. Hall Papers. Clark University Archives. Worcester, MA. By permission.

JAMES, W. 1887c, to G. S. Hall, Cambridge, MA, January 30. Hall Papers. Clark University Archives. Worcester, MA. By permission.

JAMES, W. [1895a] 1978. The knowing of things together. Reprinted in F. Burk-hardt, F. Bowers, & I. Skrupskelis, Eds. The Works of William James: Essays in Philosophy. Harvard University Press. Cambridge, MA.

JAMES, W. 1895b. Experimental psychology in America. Science. n.s. **2**: 625.

JAMES, W. 1895c, to G. Stanley Hall, Cambridge, MA, October 12. Hall Papers, Clark University Archives. Worcester, MA. By permission.

MILES, M. & C. C. MILES. 1929. Eight letters from G. Stanley Hall to H. P. Bowditch with introduction and notes. Am. J. Psychol. xvi, 327.

MURPHY, G. 1949. An Historical Introduction to Modern Psychology, 2nd ed. Harcourt, Brace. New York.

OVERSEERS RECORDS. 1871–1882. Vol. XI, p. 328. Pusey Library. Harvard University. Cambridge, MA.

PERRY, R. B. 1935. The Thought and Character of William James. 2 vols. Atlantic/Little Brown. Boston.

ROSS, D. 1972. G. Stanley Hall: The Psychologist as Prophet. University of Chicago Press. Chicago.

SIEGEL, A. W. & S. H. WHITE. 1981. The Child Study Movement: Early growth and development of the symbolized child. Ms., Harvard University. Cambridge, MA; 1982. Advan. Child Behav. Devel. **17**: 233–285.

TAYLOR, E. I. 1985. William James on Exceptional Mental States: The 1896 Unpublished Lowell Lectures. Scribner's. New York.

TAYLOR, E. I. 1985. James Jackson Putnam's fateful meeting with Freud: The 1909 Clark University Conference. In Voices: The Art and Science of Psychotherapy **21**: 1, 78–89.

TAYLOR, E. I. 1988. On the first use of 'Psychoanalysis' at the Massachusetts General Hospital, 1903–1905, J. Hist. Med. Allied Sci. **43**(4): 447–471.

TAYLOR, E. I. 1992. Psychology as a person-centered science: William James after 1890. Unpublished Ph.D. dissertation. University Professors Program. Boston University. Boston.

WHITE, S. H. 1988. Child Study at Clark University: 1894–1904. Unpublished ms. Harvard University. Cambridge, MA; 1990. J. Hist Behav. Sci. **26**: 131–150.

YERKES, R. M. 1943. The early days of comparative psychology. Psychol. Rev. **50**: 74–76.

A History of the New York Branch of the American Psychological Association, 1903–1935[a]

LUDY T. BENJAMIN, JR.

Department of Psychology
Texas A&M University
College Station, Texas 77843

[*The Eastern Psychological Association (EPA) held its 65th annual meeting in 1994. The numbering of those meetings began with a meeting of the New York Branch of the American Psychological Association in 1930, but the roots of the EPA are much deeper, beginning with the formation of the New York Branch in 1903. The branch began as a forum for the exchange of scientific information in psychology in the New York City area. It was initially successful, meeting three times per year for a one-day program, and featured a Who's Who of speakers delivering some of the most important papers in the history of American psychology. After World War I its character, like that of psychology, began to change as the program reflected the growth in applied psychology and the membership began to be dominated by nonpsychologists. Its reorganization in 1930 restored control of the branch to university-based psychologists and reestablished the scientific goals that characterize the EPA today.*]

As the ninth president of the American Psychological Association (APA), midwesterner Joseph Jastrow chaired the meeting of the APA Council of Directors in Baltimore in December 1900. A principal subject of debate was the location of the APA meetings. Since its organization in 1892, the APA had held its annual meetings in Philadelphia (twice), New York (twice), Princeton, Boston, Ithaca, New Haven, and Baltimore, clearly favoring the strong northeastern base of psychology. Complaints about that regional bias came primarily from psychologists from the Midwest, who argued that it was difficult for them to attend the meetings on a regular basis.

Two decisions were made at that 1900 meeting to benefit psychologists outside of the Northeast. The first was to hold the next meeting of the APA in Chicago. The second was to propose a bylaw change that would permit the establishment of regional APA groups. At the Chicago meeting in 1901, the following bylaw change was formally adopted by the APA: "Local

[a]A slightly modified version of this paper was printed in the October 1991 issue of the *American Psychologist* and is reprinted here by permission of the American Psychological Association, Inc.

Sections. Members and Associates of the Association living in any center may, with the authorization of the Council of Directors, organize themselves into a local section for the holding of meetings" (Fernberger 1932, p. 34). Approval was given at that meeting for the founding of local sections in New York, Cambridge, and Chicago ("Proceedings of the Tenth" 1902). The Chicago Branch of the APA was the first to be established, holding its organizational meeting on the campus of Northwestern University on April 19, 1902 ("Notes and News" 1902); it is considered the predecessor of the Midwestern Psychological Association (Benjamin 1979).

The New York section, the forerunner of the Eastern Psychological Association (EPA), held its first meeting as the New York Branch of the APA on February 23, 1903, chaired by Edward L. Thorndike. A brief announcement of the meeting appeared in the *Psychological Review* ("Notes and News" 1903), and a full description of the program, written by the secretary, James E. Lough (1903a), was published in *Science.*

NEW YORK ACADEMY OF SCIENCES

Some psychologists in the New York area had been meeting regularly in a local group since 1896. At the urging of James McKeen Cattell, arrangements were made "for the more formal recognition of the mental and social sciences" ("Notes" 1896, p. 356) by the formation of a section of the New York Academy of Sciences for Anthropology, Psychology, and Philology, divided into anthropology–psychology and philology subsections. Although technically subsections, these new groups were referred to as sections. They met on the fourth Monday of each month, the initial meeting of the section on anthropology and psychology having been held on April 27, 1896. Sociologist Franklin H. Giddings was chair of the section and psychologist–anthropologist Livingston Farrand was secretary. Cattell, Giddings, Farrand, and Franz Boas read papers at the first meeting ("Notes" 1896; "Scientific Notes and News" 1896).

The anthroplogy–psychology section met six times a year, alternating months with the philology section, and combined papers in psychology and anthropology at each meeting. Dues for academy membership were high ($10.00 per year) and few psychologists actually belonged. Psychologists in the Academy, concerned about recruiting more members, agreed to hold separate meetings for psychology and anthropology (three each per year), beginning in 1902. This allowed psychologists more control over their program, but the advent of local sections of the APA offered New York area psychologists the even greater advantages of lower dues (50¢) and more involvement of younger psychologists and graduate students (Cattell 1940).

Until around 1920, meetings of the New York Branch were held in conjunction with the psychology group meetings of the New York Academy of Sciences. Following an academic calendar, the branch typically met in November, February, and April. All meetings were one-day events, except for a special two-day memorial meeting for William James in 1911.

The branch used dues primarily for printing and mailing postcard programs announcing the time and place of the meeting, the presenters, and the titles of their papers. Academy section meetings were usually held at the American Museum of Natural History, but when the psychology group began to meet separately from the anthropology group, its meetings were normally held on the campus of Columbia University, and sometimes at the Washington Square campus of New York University. These meetings were always labeled as joint meetings of the Academy section and the New York Branch (Woodworth 1941).

The chair and secretary of the Academy section were always either psychologists or anthropologists. When the officers were psychologists, they also held the same positions as officers of the psychology branch; when officers were anthropologists, the psychology branch elected its own officers. The secretary performed virtually all of the duties of the branch, including collection of dues, arrangement of the program, and preparation and mailing of the postcard meeting announcements. Robert Woodworth (1941) described the form of the branch–section meetings:

> The typical meeting in the old days (say 1905–1915) consisted of afternoon and evening sessions, with dinner between. At other times, when only an evening session was held at the Museum, the group adjourned to a near-by cafe for free discussion after the formal meeting. (p. 2)

There were five meetings of the Academy section between the December 1901 APA meeting that permitted the establishment of sections and the initial meeting of the New York Branch in 1903. It is possible that the branch was planned at one of those meetings, although there is no indication of that in the published minutes. During that time Farrand and Thorndike served as chairs of the section and Woodworth and Lough served as secretaries; thus the branch had strong support in the leadership of the section.

INITIAL MEETING OF THE NEW YORK BRANCH

Lough's (1903a) account of that first meeting summarized eight papers, two of which were read by title only. Whether Cattell had any direct involvement in planning that program is not known; however, his influence is obvious throughout. The first speaker was Yale University's Edward W.

Scripture, whose "Phonetic Surveys" described the latest technologies for voice recording; phonographs, graphophones, and gramophones.

Scripture was followed by two New York University psychologists: Lough described an illusion of movement in the background of stereoscopic pictures when they were moved from side to side, and Robert MacDougall reported his research on facial vision, arguing that auditory cues played no role in performance.

Cattell led the Columbia University contingent with a paper that discussed the accuracy with which grades could be assigned in college classes and several methods for grade assignment. Two papers were given by psychologists–anthropologists Clark Wissler and Joseph Hershey Bair of Columbia, both of whom described correlational studies of anthropometric measures in children. The lone graduate student presenter was William Harper Davis, Cattell's student, whose paper, "A Preliminary Report on Tests of One Hundred Men of Science," was read by title only. However, he was able to deliver this paper at the second meeting of the branch two months later (Lough, 1903b).

The other non–New Yorker on the program was Scripture's colleague at Yale, philosopher E. Hershey Sneath. He presented an analysis of psychology over the previous 25 years, calling attention to changes in the nature of training, the differentiation of subfields, and the development of new methods. He also commented on the growing status of psychology among the more established sciences.

STRUCTURE AND CONTENT OF THE MEETINGS

The meeting schedule for the branch changed very little over the next 20 years. The branch kept to its three-meetings-per-year schedule through 1925, even during World War I. The branch's secretaries wrote summaries of the meetings, which were usually published in *Science* or in the *Journal of Philosophy, Psychology, and Scientific Method,* and occasionally in the *Psychological Bulletin.* Cattell had some connection to all of those journals as either publisher, editor, or founder. It is interesting that no mention of the New York Branch meetings was ever made in the *American Journal of Psychology.* Many societies, including the Chicago branch of the APA, the Western Psychological Association, the Southern Society for Philosophy and Psychology, and the American Psychological Association regularly published their reports in that journal. Yet the New York Branch was absent, both in terms of a meeting report or even a short meeting announcement. Perhaps that omission was due to the hard feelings between G. Stanley Hall and Cattell that began when the latter was a graduate student with Hall at Johns Hopkins University in the 1880s.

Published accounts have been found for 42 meetings from 1903 through 1925. If the branch met three times as scheduled during each of those years there would have been a total of 69 meetings, which leaves possibly 27 meetings for which there are no published accounts. Eight of those meetings can be confirmed by unpublished documents, but the existence of the others is a mystery. However, it seems likely that they were held and not reported. Only two published accounts of the meetings appear after 1917 (in 1918 and 1921), yet meetings can be confirmed from unpublished sources for every year from 1918 through 1925 except for 1922. Perhaps the secretaries felt too burdened with other duties to prepare the meeting summaries for publication three times a year.

TABLE 1 is a frequency analysis of the programs by topic for the first 15 years of the branch (1903–1917), summarized in 5-year intervals. The number of papers in most categories is so small as to make any trend analyses suspect. Still, the declines in philosophy and sensation–perception and the increases in learning and the applied areas reflect broader trends in American psychology during that period. Published summaries or unpublished programs are rare after 1917, making frequency tables for those years difficult to compile.

According to the published and unpublished accounts of the meetings

TABLE 1. Papers Presented to the New York Branch of the American Psychological Association by Topic (1903–1917)

Topic	1903–1907		1908–1912		1913–1917	
	No.	%	No.	%	No.	%
Sensation–perception	27	31.4	16	18.0	5	7.2
Philosophy	21	24.4	15	16.9	3	4.3
Mental testing	16	18.6	10	11.2	14	20.3
Educational psychology	4	4.6	1	1.1	4	5.8
Apparatus–methodology	3	3.5	1	1.1	2	2.9
Language–thought	3	3.5	2	2.2	1	1.4
Physiological psychology	3	3.5	3	3.5	3	4.3
Clinical psychology	2	2.3	7	7.9	7	10.1
Learning	2	2.3	12	13.5	9	13.0
Memory	2	2.3	5	5.6	10	14.5
Comparative psychology	1	1.2	2	2.2	1	1.4
Developmental psychology	1	1.2	1	1.1	2	2.9
Social psychology	1	1.2	1	1.1	1	1.4
Fatigue	—	—	5	5.6	—	—
Industrial psychology	—	—	5	5.6	3	4.3
Motor processes	—	—	3	3.4	4	5.8
Motivation–emotion	—	—	—	—	2	2.9

from 1903 through 1925, the format of the meetings remained essentially unchanged from the initial meeting until 1915. The one-day meeting usually involved the presentation of four papers before dinner and another four after. By 1915, the afternoon sessions were no longer held; meetings usually began with a dinner, followed by a session involving two to four papers. The reduction in meeting time may have been due to waning interest in the meetings, or the result of growing concern about the war in Europe. The meetings were in New York City, except in 1903 and 1907, when they were in New Haven, and in 1906 and 1914, when they were in Princeton.

The programs were not arranged around a single theme or even several themes. Instead, the norm was diversity, similar to that exhibited in the program of the first meeting. The two exceptions were a 1911 meeting that featured a number of papers on William James and a 1915 meeting that consisted of five papers dealing with the conditions affecting efficiency (Poffenberger 1915; Woodworth 1911).

One or two graduate students were usually among the presenters at most meetings of the branch, whereas they were not permitted to present at the Academy meetings. Among these students was Naomi Norsworthy, who presented her research on mentally deficient children at the March 1904 meeting. Her address, which described the results of the testing of 150 children in state institutions for the "feeble minded" as well as special classes in the New York City schools, was the first presentation by a woman at a branch meeting (Lough 1904).

The bulk of the program was made up of university faculty members, with the heaviest representation from Columbia University and New York University. Columbia's Cattell, Thorndike, and Woodworth were frequent presenters. It was at these meetings that Cattell described his research on the measurement of scientific merit, Thorndike described his work on the variability of mental traits, and Woodworth described his work on mental testing, based on the testing program he conducted at the 1904 St. Louis Exposition.

Some programs, such as the third meeting of 1903, held at Yale University in conjunction with the Philosophical Club of Yale, were particularly star-studded. Presenters included Lightner Witmer and seven past or future APA presidents: Cattell, Woodworth, Henry Rutgers Marshall, Charles H. Judd, Raymond Dodge, Robert Yerkes, and Shepherd Ivory Franz. This meeting was also unusual in the number of universities represented in the program: Dartmouth, Yale, Harvard, Wesleyan, the University of Pennsylvania, and Columbia.

The New York City meetings frequently included out-of-town guests on the program. Sometimes these guests were scheduled as part of the branch's program; examples include John Watson's talk on vision and Henry Herbert Goddard's address on the heritability of mental traits, both in 1911. At other times these speakers were part of a university-sponsored program in the city, and their addresses were incorporated into the branch's program; these included Edward Bradford Titchener's lecture at Columbia University in 1908 on the laws of attention.

The early published program summaries included brief abstracts of the talks. Over the years the length of those abstracts increased until they averaged one to one and a half printed pages, yet they contained little more than a description of the addresses presented. Occasionally some of the discussion following the address would be included, even identifying by name participants who raised particular points, but that was the exception. Sometimes the remarks were quite cryptic: The description of Goddard's 1911 address concluded with the sentence, "Considerable discussion followed" (Hollingworth 1912). One is left to wonder what was said in reaction to his presentation of the data that would form the basis of his book on the Kallikaks, published the following year.

If discussions other than those involving the program occurred, they were never reported in the published reports. Apparently such business activities as the election of officers took place at these meetings, but the secretaries reported only the program. Such a focus was typical of the reports of other academic societies appearing in the scientific journals; however, several of these other groups also reported their business news. Whether the branch was involved in other activities is mostly unknown. Robert Woodworth addressed this issue in a 1925 letter:

Only once, I think, has the branch taken any action aside from its scientific program and the election of its own officers. One time it adopted a resolution in support of some movement or other—something, I believe, in the direction of promoting clinical psychology. The resolution was introduced at one of the regular scientific meetings and passed, and was then used in support of the movement in question. (p. 1)

No trace of that resolution has been found. It is possible that it was a resolution to support the formation of the American Association of Clinical Psychologists in 1917 or its subsequent inclusion within the formal structure of the APA. Columbia University's Leta Hollingworth and several other New Yorkers were prominently involved in that organization and may have encouraged the branch to support that effort (Napoli 1981). Another possibility is that the resolution supported the New York State Association of Consulting Psychologists, which was founded in 1921 for the purposes of "the promotion of high standards of professional qualifications for consulting, psychologists [and] stimulating research work in the field of psychological analysis and evaluation" ("Notes and News" 1921, p. 439). Both Leta

Hollingworth and Robert Woodworth were members of the executive committee of this group. However, if the resolution had been about this group, surely Woodworth would have remembered it, both because of his direct involvement and because of its recency.

Arguably the most important address presented at the branch (perhaps the most important address ever presented at any psychological meeting) was John B. Watson's "Psychology as the Behaviorist Views It," which was delivered on February 24, 1913. The summary of that meeting did not include an abstract of the paper because by the time the summary appeared, Watson's address was already in print as part of the March 1913 issue of the *Psychological Review*. Nor is there any indication of reaction to the paper (Hollingworth 1913). Apparently people were not lining up to react to Watson, as no related papers were presented in later branch meetings. This lack of published reaction supports Franz Samelson's (1981) conclusions that support for and criticisms of Watsonian behaviorism were slow in materializing. However, Watson's address was not the first discussion of behaviorism at the branch. Columbia's William P. Montague presented a paper on April 24, 1911, entitled "Has Psychology Lost Its Mind?" The meeting summary described that paper as follows:

The movement to dispense with the concept of mind or consciousness and to substitute the concept of behavior as the sufficient object of psychological study was criticized (1) on the ground of ambiguity, (2) on the ground of inadequacy. (Hollingworth 1911, p. 494)

Montague attacked a psychology that sought to describe consciousness solely in terms of a one-to-one correspondence between stimulus events and motor responses. As in the case of Watson's later presentation, no reactions to this address are indicated, and subsequent programs did not follow up on the theme.

REORGANIZATION OF THE NEW YORK BRANCH

After World I, psychology's popularity rose dramatically, leading Canadian humorist Stephen Leacock (1924) to declare that America was suffering from an "outbreak of psychology" (p. 471). Popular magazines sprang up in the early 1920s to sell psychology to the public, and daily newspaper columnists declared that everyone needed the services of psychologists to achieve the greatest happiness and success (Benjamin 1986). Public demand for psychological services was great and there were simply not enough psychologists available to meet that demand. Consequently, many individuals with little or no psychological training began to advertise their services as psychologists, which led the APA to establish a certification program for psychologists in the 1920s. The program certified only about 25 psychologists and was abandoned after a few years. The New York State Association of Consulting Psychologists, mentioned earlier, also attempted to identify qualified psychological practitioners for the public. However, in the absence of any state statutes, this organization, like the APA, was powerless to stop the practice of psychology by individuals with dubious credentials. Not surprisingly, these societal changes affected the New York Branch.

Three Columbia University psychologists served as secretaries of the branch during the 1920s. However, they did not submit any program summaries for publication in the journals, and no unpublished accounts have been found. The only verification of the meetings in the 1920s are some program postcards and occasional references in the correspondence of psychologists of that time. When compared with earlier programs, those of the 1920s show an increase in the presentation of applied research, such as evaluation of military troops, selection of salespeople, and study of human factors in automobile accidents. This shift was to be expected given the activities of psychologists during the war. In fact, applied papers had been increasing in the programs before the war, but that increase accelerated after 1918. This change, coupled with the growth of educational, clinical, and industrial psychology in applied settings, alarmed some members of the branch who felt that the association was in danger of abandoning its original purpose as a forum for scientific exchange.

The most significant change in the New York Branch during the 1920s was in the membership of the organization. Because the branch had no bylaws or membership requirements (other than the payment of dues), virtually anyone could belong to the branch. According to the 1901 APA bylaw change that established the branches, they were supposed to be made up of members and associates of the APA. However, the New York Branch did not conform to that requirement. A membership roll of the branch in 1925 lists 150 members, only 40 of whom also belonged to APA; most of the others were probably ineligible to join APA (FIG. 1). These other branch members were psychiatrists, educators, ministers, sociologists, graduate students, and a large number who cannot be identified. Undoubtedly some of them were laypersons practicing psychology and using their branch membership as a credential.

By the end of the 1920s there was considerable concern among legitimate psychologists over the viability of the branch. Indeed, some of the most visible psychologists in the area had stopped attending the meetings, perhaps because of the changes in membership, but also because of the growing applied and consulting emphases of the program. For several years, Henry Garrett, secretary of the branch in 1929, had difficulty in arranging the program because of growing dissatisfaction among the psychologist

NEW YORK BRANCH

OF

The American Psychological Association

1924-1925

THE NEW YORK BRANCH of the American Psychological Association will meet on Monday, April 27th, at 8 P. M., in Room 305, Schermerhorn Hall, Columbia University.

DR. LILLIAN M. GILBRETH,
"Motion Study and Psychology."

DR. BESS V. CUNNINGHAM,
"A Report of Studies of Pre-school Children'

DR. HENRY C. LINK,
"An Experiment in the Selection of Salesmen."

PROFESSOR ANATHON AALL,
"The Problem of Animal Mind."
(Illustrated with lantern slides).

PROF. W. B. PILLSBURY will preside.

H. K. NIXON, *Secretary-Treasurer,*
Columbia University.

MEMBERSHIP ROLL, 1925

The New York Branch of the American Psychological Association

Harold H. Abelson
Theodora Mead Able
*Edith Mulhall Achilles
Paul Achilles
Mary G. Allerton
Katherine Alston
Clairette P. Armstrong
Thaddeus H. Ames
Ann Anthony
*Ada H. Arlitt
Harriet S. B. Babcock
Bernice E. Barrows
A. G. Batten
*J. Carleton Bell
C. E. Benson
*W. V. Bingham
*†Grace E. Bird
*Phyllis Blanchard
Frances Blumenthal
*Frederick G. Bonser
Eleanor E. Boyakin
L. S. Brady
E. M. Burdich
Emily T. Burr
Leda B. Cady
Fred Caiola
†Edith Carothers
*†James McKeen Cattell
*George A. Coe
Sidney A. Cook
Katharine S. Day
*Geo. VanNess Dearborn
Constance Dowd
Fannie W. Dunn
Edna J. Fox
Richard B. Franken
Max Freyd
Herbert M. Garn
*Georgina S. Gates
*Arthur I. Gates
*Franklin Henry Giddings
*Lillian M. Gilbreth
Charles M. Gill
Irene L. Glenn
Bernard Glueck

B. Goldberg
Edward B. Green
Henry J. Gross
Harold M. Grossman
Ruth Lewy Guinzburg
*J. Victor Haberman
*Thomas H. Haines
*Frederick Hansen
George W. Hartmann
*†Samuel B. Heckman
Georgene Hoffman
*H. L. Hollingworth
Smith Ely Jelliffe
Thomas Jenkins
A. M. Johanson
Jane S. Joliffe
K. S. Kao
Harriet H. Keith
C. M. Kelly
William H. Kilpatrick
W. B. Kittredge
Paul Klapper
Natalie Kneeland
*Christine Ladd-Franklin
*Herbert S. Langfeld
George A. Layng
Agnes B. Leahy
Kate Lewis
*Henry C. Link
*†James E. Lough
*Howard D. Marsh
*Henry Rutgers Marshall
Dorothea M. Marston
Warren S. McCulloch
Helen Meyer
George M. Michaels
*David Mitchell
*Gardner Murphy
*Sante Naccarati
†Margaret E. Noonan
G. F. Orphal
Joseph Millard Osman
*Arthur S. Otis
Margaret Otis
Alice E. Paulsen

*John Pickett Turner
E. H. Tyndale
Mary B. M. Uxem
Elizabeth F. Vilkomerson
Elizabeth A. Walsh
*Carl J. Warden
*Howard C. Warren
James Weinland
*F. L. Wells
B. Wells
*Mary T. Whitley
A. E. Wiggam
Mrs. A. E. Wiggam
*F. J. Woodbridge
*R. S. Woodworth

*Rudolph Pintner
*A. T. Poffenberger
*Louise E. Poull
Dorothy Rennie
*David Edgar Rice
Dorothy C. Rowell
Louise L. Schriefer
Harry M. Schulman
L. Shepherd
Myra E. Shimberg
H. B. Silsbee
P. D. Stout
S. A. Tannenbaum
Frederick Tilney
Katherine Treat

* Member of the American Psychological Association.
† Dues paid 1924-1926.

FIGURE 1. Program of a 1925 Meeting of the New York Branch of the American Psychological Association.

members. His frustration was shared by Douglas Fryer (1940a) of New York University, who described the situation as follows:

Those with serious interests in the science of psychology felt that the New York Branch as it was conceived during the previous decade had served all too inadequately the professional interests of psychologists in the area centering around New York City. (p. 1)

In an effort to change this situation, Elaine Kinder (the membership chair) and Fryer (the incoming secretary–treasurer) identified 360 psychologists living within 100 miles of New York City. They mailed invitations as far north as Albany, as far east as New Haven, and as far south as Philadelphia, for a one-day meeting of an interim organization to be held April 12, 1930, on the Heights campus of New York University. An overwhelming 240 of the 360 who were invited actually attended.

The program for the 1930 meeting consisted of 31 papers presented successively in six sessions. One of the sessions was on applied and industrial psychology and consisted of five papers, four of them from university professors and one from a psychologist with the Personnel Research Federation of New York City. There was also a session of six papers on consulting psychology. Of the presenters, three were psychologists, and the professional identity of the others cannot be determined; only one of the six worked at a university. The other sessions were on general psychology, experimental psychology, animal psychology, and child and genetic psychology. All of the presenters in those sessions held university positions (*Spring Meeting* 1930).

The eight-person program committee for the 1930 meeting was chaired by Garrett and included Clark Hull and Ernest Wever. The program listed the New York State Association of Consulting Psychologists as a participating organization, and that organization was undoubtedly responsible for the session on consulting psychology. Woodworth was named honorary president and addressed the more than 100 psychologists who attended the dinner that evening. It is from this meeting that the current Eastern Psychological Association numbers its meetings.

At the business meeting, Fryer asked the group to decide whether it wanted a scientific organization. A motion to that effect was introduced from the floor and was approved unanimously. It was decided that the organization would be called the New York Branch of the APA and that the group would ask the APA council of directors to confirm its existence, which the APA did at its December 1930 meeting.

The group decided to hold annual meetings in the spring. Howard C. Warren was elected president for the 1931 meeting at Columbia University, and an executive committee, consisting of Warren, Fryer, Kinder, Garrett, Hull, and Albert T. Poffenberger, Jr., was appointed to serve until bylaws could be drafted and approved (Fryer 1940b).

No report of the 1930 meeting was published, but a 21-page report of the 1931 meeting appeared in the *Psychological Bulletin,* marking the first published report of the branch in 10 years ("Proceedings of the New York Branch" 1931). The bylaws of the reorganized branch were unanimously adopted at that meeting, defining much of the contemporary structure of the Eastern Psychological Association. Membership was restricted to members and associates of the APA in good standing who were located within a 100-mile radius of New York City. Nonmembers could attend the meetings, but could not present papers unless they were sponsored by a member. Psychology graduate students were encouraged to participate and to become APA associates and branch members.

There was concern among the branch's leadership about the content of the program. It was agreed that in arranging the annual program, there should be no discrimination between "pure and applied research, but it was to be understood that scientific papers meant experimental results" (Fryer 1940b, p. 7). That concern was formalized in a resolution unanimously approved at the 1931 meeting:

> That no distinction be made in the scientific programs of the New York Branch between pure and applied psychology; that the Association emphasize the presentation of experimental (including mental measurement) research whether performed with pure or applied intent; that research performed with either intent be included in sections arranged according to *scientific* fields of research. To avoid duplication of the activities of the Association of Consulting Psychologists it is recommended that papers dealing with consulting practice be presented at the meetings of that Association or some similar body. ("Proceedings of the New York Branch" 1931, p. 615)

The annual program was placed in the hands of a three-person program committee established by the bylaws and appointed by the board of directors. The bylaws called for the committee to "conduct and supervise the scientific programs of the Branch" ("Proceedings of the New York Branch" 1931, p. 619).

The new bylaws solved the membership problems by excluding nonpsychologists, but they also excluded the consulting psychologists. The New York State Association of Consulting Psychologists was not listed in the 1931 program; there was no session on consulting psychology, nor was there a single presentation by a psychologist not affiliated with a university. The members of the branch had voted to narrow its program domain—psychologists who were not presenting the results of experimental investigations were not welcome. Consulting psychologists withdrew to their own organization.

The reorganized New York Branch of the APA continued to meet once a year in the pattern of the 1930 meeting and to publish reports annually in the *Psychological Bulletin*. The branch began numbering its meetings with the 1932 meeting at the University of Pennsylvania, designating it the "Third Spring Meeting" of the branch. The "metropolitans" (those members residing in New York City) and the "outlanders" agreed that meetings should be held outside the city in alternate years. Accordingly, the group met in New Haven in 1933 and in Princeton in 1935, and in New York City in 1934 and 1936.

THE QUESTION OF AFFILIATION WITH THE APA

While the branch was in the midst of reorganizing itself to preserve its identity as a scientific association for psychologists, some members were concerned about how best to accomplish that in terms of the branch's relationship to the APA. Members who favored identity as a branch of the APA felt that the APA should organize branches throughout the United States, allocating territory to each branch. Psychologists beyond the 100-mile radius of New York City were already complaining about their exclusion from the New York branch when they had no other regional association to which they could belong. Those opposing continuation as a branch cited the membership restrictions imposed by the APA and the lack of a separate identity for the organization. They noted the decision in 1928 of the former Chicago Branch of the APA to establish itself as the Midwestern Psychological Association, independent of APA and its membership requirements. Other regional groups, such as the Southern Society for Philosophy and Psychology, had remained independent of the APA, and new groups were being established in the 1930s as independent organizations, such as the Psychometric Society, the Society for the Psychological Study of Social Issues, and the American Association for Applied Psychology.

The New York Branch acted on the territory issue at its 1936 meeting at Fordham University, changing the name of the organization to the Eastern Branch of the APA. Its territory was to include all of the Atlantic seaboard. The 1936 annual report interpreted the territory as follows: "It may draw its membership from Florida to Canada, and westward to contiguous territory of whatever branch of the American Psychological Association may exist or may be formed" (Rogers 1936, p. 467). As an immediate result, membership increased from 268 in 1937 to 393 in 1938.

Disagreement about branches of the APA led the APA council of directors to discontinue them in 1936. Concurrently, the APA bylaws were changed to allow for the affiliation of regional associations. These regional affiliates were permitted to define their own memberships, but they were not allowed to seek affiliate status unless a majority of their members were also APA members (*By-laws* 1937).

As a result of the changes, the Midwestern Psychological Association requested affiliation with the APA in 1937, which was granted in September 1938 (Olson 1938). Also in 1938, the Eastern Branch voted to change its name to Eastern Psychological Association, thus establishing an identity independent of the APA, although it retained the APA affiliate status it had held since 1930 and continued to require membership in the APA for its own members. Thus the New York Branch, in existence for approximately 35 years, was subsumed in the new Eastern Psychological Association, which celebrated its 65th annual meeting in 1994. That numerical designation begins with the annual spring meetings in 1930 and thus includes six meetings under the title of the New York Branch and two meetings as the Eastern Branch of the APA, yet it completely ignores the 50 earlier meetings that can be documented between 1903 and 1925. Officers of the branch from 1903 to 1935 are shown in TABLE 2.

TABLE 2. Officers of the New York Branch of the APA

Year	Chair[a]	Secretary-Treasurer
1903–1904	Edward L. Thorndike	James E. Lough
1905	Frederick J. E. Woodbridge	James E. Lough
1906–1907	Robert MacDougall	Robert S. Woodworth
1908–1910	Adolf Meyer	Robert S. Woodworth
1911–1912	Robert S. Woodworth	Harry L. Hollingworth
1913–1914	Wendell T. Bush	Harry L. Hollingworth[c]
1915–1918[b]	—	Albert Poffenberger, Jr.
1919–1920[b]	—	F. Edith Carothers
1921–1922[b]	—	Edith M. Achilles
1923–1925[b]	—	Howard K. Nixon
1926–1929[b]	—	Henry E. Garrett
1930	Robert S. Woodworth	Douglas Fryer
1931	Howard C. Warren	Douglas Gryer
1932	Margaret Floy Washburn	Paul S. Achilles
1933	Raymond Dodge	Paul S. Achilles
1934	James McKeen Cattell	Paul S. Achilles
1935	Joseph Jastrow	Herbert W. Rogers

[a]Title was changed to Honorary President in 1930.

[b]Chairs are unknown from 1915 to 1929, although the following were listed as "presiding" at a meeting during that time: Robert MacDougall (1924), Robert S. Woodworth (1925), Walter B. Pillsbury (1925).

[c]Served as acting Secretary-Treasurer during part of 1918.

LEGACY OF THE NEW YORK BRANCH

Although the New York Branch has been officially extinct for nearly 60 years, the philosophy of its founders is very much embodied in the contemporary philosophy of the Eastern Psychological Association. The EPA exists exclusively to conduct annual meetings for the exchange of scientific information. That was the commitment of the branch, and it has been reaffirmed in a number of decisions throughout the history of the branch and the EPA (Lane 1961). Furthermore, both the branch and the EPA have fostered the scientific development of graduate students in psychology by encouraging them to present papers at the meetings.

Although other organizations in psychology may have multiple purposes, the EPA has adhered to a rather rigid interpretation of its mission in the dissemination of the science of psychology. Like the branch, which defined that mission, the EPA has eschewed activities that would carry it beyond its original purposes, with the possible exception of the development of a job placement service. Its adoption of resolutions has been minimal, and most of those approved have had to do with the freedom of scientific inquiry and expression. Like its predecessor, the EPA has not seen itself as an organization to engage in social or political activism.

Gorham Lane (1961) understood that the history of the EPA included the history of the earliest years of the New York Branch, although his article included only a single page on the branch's history. That brief attention to the branch and the practice of numbering the EPA meetings from 1930 may make us forget the continuity of purpose and setting. The purpose of this article is to expand the historical record and make accessible the history of the New York Branch of the APA.

REFERENCES

BENJAMIN, L. T., JR. 1979. The Midwestern Psychological Association: A history of the organization and its antecedents, 1902–1978. Am. Psychol. **34**: 201–213.
BENJAMIN, L. T., JR. 1986. Why don't they understand us? A history of psychology's public image. Am. Psychol. **41**: 941–946.
By-laws of the American Psychological Association (revision). 1937. *In* Willard C. Olson Papers, American Psychological Association Archives, Library of Congress, Washington, DC.
CATTELL, J. M. 1940. Letter to Douglas Fryer (February 6). *In* Eastern Psychological Association Archives, Archives of the History of American Psychology, University of Akron, Akron, OH.
FERNBERGER, S. W. 1932. The American Psychological Association: A historical summary, 1892–1930. Psychol. Bull. **29**: 1–89.
FRYER, D. 1940a. Decade 1930–1939. *In* Eastern Psychological Association Archives, Archives of the History of American Psychology, University of Akron, Akron, OH.

FRYER, D. 1940b. The social behavior of eastern psychologists: Historical sketch of the Eastern Psychological Association: Decade 1929–1939. *In* Eastern Psychological Association Archives, Archives of the History of American Psychology, University of Akron, Akron, OH.

HOLLINGWORTH, H. L. 1911. New York Branch of the American Psychological Association. J. Phil. Psychol. Sci. Method **8**: 491–496.

HOLLINGWORTH, H. L. 1912. The New York Branch of the American Psychological Association. J. Phil. Psychol. Sci. Method **9**: 234–238.

HOLLINGWORTH, H. L. 1913. The New York Branch of the American Psychological Association. J. Phil. Psychol. Sci. Method **10**: 270–274.

LANE, G. 1961. The Eastern Psychological Association: 1896–1960. Am. Psychol. **16**: 249–255.

LEACOCK, S. 1924. A manual for the new mentality. Harpers March: 471–480.

LOUGH, J. E. 1903a. New York Academy of Sciences. Science **17**: 588–590.

LOUGH, J. E. 1903b. New York Academy of Sciences Section on Anthropology and Psychology. Science **18**: 81–82.

LOUGH, J. E. 1904. The New York Academy of Sciences Section on Anthropology and Psychology. J. Phil. Psychol. Sci. Method **1**: 325–328.

NAPOLI, D. S. 1981. Architects of Adjustment: The History of the Psychological Profession in the United States. Kennikat Press. Port Washington, NY.

Notes. 1896. Psychol. Rev. **3**: 356.

Notes and News. 1902. Psychol. Rev. **9**: 432.

Notes and News. 1903. Psychol. Rev. **10**: 224.

Notes and News. 1921. Psychol. Bull. **18**: 439, 568.

OLSON, W. C. 1938. Letter to J. P. Guilford (October 4). *In* Midwestern Psychological Association Archives, Archives of the History of American Psychology, University of Akron, Akron, OH.

POFFENBERGER, A. T., JR. 1915. The New York Branch of the American Psychological Association. J. Phil. Psychol. Sci. Method **12**: 243–247.

Proceedings of the New York Branch of the American Psychological Association, Inc., New York City, April, 1931. 1931. Psychol. Bull. **28**: 613–633.

Proceedings of the Tenth Annual Meeting of the American Psychological Association. 1902. Psychol. Rev. **9**: 134–155.

ROGERS, H. W. 1936. The Eastern Branch of the American Psychological Association. Science **83**: 467–468.

SAMELSON, F. 1981. Struggle for scientific authority: The reception of Watson's behaviorism. J. Hist. Behav. Sci. **17**: 399–425.

Scientific Notes and News. 1896. Science **3**: 402–403.

Spring Meeting (program). 1930. New York Branch of the American Psychological Association. *In* Eastern Psychological Association Archives, Archives of the History of American Psychology, University of Akron, Akron, OH.

WATSON, J. B. 1913. Psychology as the behaviorist views it. Psychol. Rev. **20**: 158–177.

WOODWORTH, R. S. 1911. New York Branch of the American Psychological Association. J. Phil. Psychol. Sci. Method **8**: 460–467.

WOODWORTH, R. S. 1925. Letter to F. Lyman Wells (May 8). *In* Eastern Psychological Association Archives, Archives of the History of American Psychology, University of Akron, Akron, OH.

WOODWORTH, R. S. 1941. Eastern Psychological Association: Notes on its early history (or prehistory). *In* Eastern Psychological Association Archives, Archives of the History of American Psychology, University of Akron, Akron, OH.

Joseph Jastrow: Pioneer Psychologist Facing the "Administrative Peril"

ARTHUR L. BLUMENTHAL

1180 Midland Avenue
Bronxville, New York 10708

In a research project commissioned by the University of Wisconsin in 1988, I investigated the life and career of Joseph Jastrow, founder of the Wisconsin psychology laboratory in 1888 and organizer of the large and influential Psychology Pavilion at the 1893 World's Fair in Chicago. Over the course of his life Jastrow won wide recognition among both the general public as well as academic circles. This recognition was in no small degree due to his uncanny ability as a florid writer, a lecturer, and later a radio commentator. Numerous pioneer accomplishments in psychology are also credited to his name, including the honor of earning the first American doctorate degree in psychology (Johns Hopkins, 1886). For a fuller review of Jastrow's life, see the summary of the Wisconsin University psychology centenary report in Kimble, Wertheimer, and White (1991). In the present paper I will but briefly summarize his career and then will take a closer look at one preoccupation, or distraction, that severely affected that career. It was, to use his words, "the administrative peril in education."

In growing up as the son of an internationally distinguished Talmudic scholar in a culturally rich family and in being groomed for the rabbinate from an early age, Jastrow entered the expanding world of late nineteenth century American education with an obviously distinctive shape already impressed upon his life. His was a multilingual childhood, and his cultural development was apparently enriched in a family atmosphere of European intellectual values. The family was of German origins, not Polish, as is mistakenly claimed in the brief accounts of Jastrow's life to have appeared in reviews of the history of American psychology. Joseph happened to have been born during a brief family visit to Warsaw shortly before the family emigrated. Long before then, his father had been briefly prominent in helping to lead the Polish rebellion against Russian rule.

Joseph was a precocious student whose undergraduate curriculum had been accelerated at the University of Pennsylvania, which graduated him with honors and prizes. He took the philosophy of Leibniz as the subject of his prize oration at the commencement. Typical of the immigrant rabbinical family of the turn of the century, the rabbi's son was lured into an academic career, adopted liberal, sometimes even antireligious views, and then suf-

79

fered a painful break with the distinguished, authoritarian, Old World father. Perhaps that father-son conflict, in Jastrow's case, was still being played out, symbolically, years later when he confronted and challenged the authoritarian and censorious face of the new, or redefined, institution of the American university presidency. But I would not want to become more psychoanalytic than that in this paper because the circumstances of Jastrow's administrative confrontations were shared by numerous friends and professorial associates at the turn of the century, and they were individuals who came from every sort of background and family.

Although he was America's first home-cultivated Ph.D. psychologist, although he carried laudatory letters of reference from his two distinguished mentors, G. Stanley Hall and C. S. Peirce, and although he was the author of a rapidly growing list of frequently cited publications, Jastrow had a rather difficult time (involving two years of searching) in finding a faculty position anywhere in the expanding world of American higher education. President Charles Adams at Cornell, for one example, apparently decided to delay the founding of the Cornell psychology department rather than hire Jastrow. The following are possible reasons for Jastrow's situation. One reason may be antisemitism. Another may be that Jastrow lacked the prestige of a European degree, certainly also a compelling factor, particularly when considered together with the antisemitism of a century ago. Though harder to judge, perhaps another may have been Jastrow's youth. He had completed the Ph.D. at age 23 and at that time projected an extremely youthful appearance; but on the other hand, so did the successful, yet boyish looking, young Cattell who pioneered psychology at Columbia.

The new University of Wisconsin, however, developed a pattern of hiring the bearers of Ph.D.s granted under Johns Hopkins' new Ph.D. program in the 1880s, which at that time was under the artful and humane leadership of its scholarly president Daniel Gilman, who as Jastrow fondly recalled had stressed men over bricks and mortar. It was the country's first such advanced degree program. In that context, Jastrow accepted a position originally titled "Professor of Experimental and Comparative Psychology." The title changed a decade later as he withdrew from experimental work and had accomplished little in comparative studies. While accepting the position and moving to the frontier area of Madison, Wisconsin, he remained painfully aware of how remote it was, in his view, from civilization. For as long as he could keep up his spirits in view of his situation and the troubles that were accumulating for him in Madison, Jastrow expended exceptional energy and apparently all of his personal resources to import "culture" into Wisconsin. The "Palace of Culture" he erected on the edge of the Wisconsin campus still stands. In 1988, when I was able to pay a visit, it was occupied by a secretive religious cult. Of course I found that the artwork, the lavish imported carpets and furnishings, the string quartets, and the visiting intellectuals from Europe that I had read of in turn-of-century notices were long gone, but still the size of the rooms, the woodwork, and the stairways echoed an elegant past. It was to me a delightful happenstance, when in Madison, to encounter a couple of local octogenarians who had known Jastrow and who still chuckled over his having built a palace for himself that had been even more elegant than the home of the university president (Charles Adams in the 1890s).

Before pursuing the implications of that last observation, let us first locate Jastrow in the world of psychology. His graduate work at Johns Hopkins had focused on the themes of psychophysics and reaction-time studies, or the core topics of the experimental psychology of that day. Jastrow's work brought him instant recognition, particularly his discovery of subliminal effects in psychophysical judgments. That finding bore, perhaps, the germ of the most important theme of his life's work in psychology—the effects of subtle stimuli and barely conscious processes on self-control and beliefs. Still his publications roamed widely over all topics that were current in psychology at the turn of the century. He had been hired as professor of experimental and comparative psychology. And at first he threw himself into experimental work, being relatively less concerned with comparative psychology, which in that time had a broader meaning that included developmental psychology, comparisons of aboriginal mental processes, and animal behavior. His life vis-à-vis experimental psychology was soon to parallel that of William James. Both men had been early enthusiasts of the new experimentalism in the field; but both quickly discovered that they were temperamentally unsuited to it and abandoned it. Jastrow, however, continued to sponsor it through students at Wisconsin.

In accordance with the central and continuing theme of his writings, that of subtle influences upon self-control, he introduced research on hypnosis at Wisconsin and for many years taught a course on medical hypnosis in the Wisconsin medical school. Later he turned the course over to his most illustrious graduate student, Clark Hull, who had by 1930 developed the study of hypnosis into a refined experimental technology, reflecting the mechanistic style and the precision of Hull's later accomplishments in learning theory. But those latter developments were anathema to Jastrow's Jamesian temperament. In most matters of style and personal interest, Jastrow and Hull could not have been more different.

One especially important contribution to the American public's recognition of psychology came from Jastrow's organization and administration of the Psychology Pavilion at the World's Fair (the Columbian Exposition) at Chicago in 1893. He arranged for the import and display, for the first time to a large American audience, of the best of the world's new experimental psychology as well as a special section devoted to developmental psychology. It involved mostly the European artifacts of the field—representations of the best of early work, laboratories, and instrumentation. He used the facilities of the Fair to collect a massive amount of psychophysical and reaction-time data on thousands of subjects who passed through. The whole project was patterned after Galton's slightly earlier and similar work in England. It was at this site that Jastrow met the young Helen Keller and gave her the first systematic tests of her abilities; he had earlier carried out research on the dreams of the blind, which is still cited today. The amount of effort that Jastrow devoted to the organization and administration of this spectacle was enormous. Yet the Wisconsin university president had obstinately refused to release him from his classes for that year, and so he was forced to run back and forth between Madison and Chicago for the duration of the Fair. By 1894 he was exhausted and fell victim to a seriously illness which forced him to take a long medical leave from teaching for over a year.

Jastrow's most widely read and most reprinted book was *Fact And Fable In Psychology* (1901), a collection of essays that debunks a number of pop psychology beliefs in the context of illustrating how subtle events and forces that swirl around us can deflect our judgment and unknowingly distort perceptions and other mental processes. The theme of self-control again animated the 1906 book *The Subconscious.* Except for his popular critical book, *The House That Freud Built,* the eight books he wrote in the 1930s were directed entirely at the popular audience and were prescriptions for better self-control. He was also a prolific contributor to popular magazines throughout his life. It is noteworthy that although he supported the first appearance on the psychological horizon of John Watson's behaviorism, he quickly reversed his position in the 1920s and filled the periodical press with polemical attacks on it. Examples can be found in *The Saturday Review* (Jastrow 1928) or in *The American Scholar* (Jastrow 1935). In the latter article he concludes as follows: "A science that can endure the ravages of two such distempers as behaviorism and psychoanalysis without permanent disfigurement must have a lusty constitution" (p. 269).

One aspect of Jastrow's barbs against both behaviorism and Freudianism was the argument that they were becoming movements of an essentially religious or cultish character. That view was part of another lifelong theme— the critique of cults of all sorts. He was, for example, frequently caught up in public clashes with the newer American religious movements (e.g., Christian Scientists and Mormons) and also with faith healers, theosophists, mind readers, spiritists, and others. On a moment's reflection you will find this concern to represent, actually, not a separate theme, but simply an extension of the one theme of the subtle deflections and distortions of human consciousness and self-control that we are all constantly susceptible to.

Jastrow was nothing if not a writer. His was a style of writing that was developed in the nineteenth century. It was Victorian and florid. If you approach it with the attitude that you are about to read a lavish imitator of, say, the novelist Henry James, you will be in a more advantageous position than the experimental psychologist of a later period, not trained in the history of literature, who might occasionally pick up one of Jastrow's books. To illustrate this point concisely (and I hope tellingly), let me cite a remark in a review of Jastrow's book *The Subconscious*. The review was written by Jastrow's early behavioristic colleague Knight Dunlap, whose style, as a product of the era, exemplifies the same faults he criticizes in Jastrow.

> The treatise throughout is furnished with a wealth of illustration which may be of use to the instructing psychologist, but it is embellished with a profusion of metaphor, simile and analogy, which, under the author's mastery of polysyllabic verbiage, gives rise to a florid fluency apt to cause the newly introduced reader to lose the path of the argument amidst the rhetorical gardens which surround it. (Dunlap 1907, 848)

Yet while at first appearing pompous and stuffy, Jastrow's writings are filled with a type of humor, suitable to his genre, in which I find the strains of Mark Twain. For instance,

> Returning some years ago from a prolonged sojourn abroad, I was on the watch for the first convincing incident that would reflect the American trait. Emerging from the attentions of the customs officials, who lost no time in showing me my place in their scheme of existence, I was accosted at the gates of liberty by a foreign urchin with the breezy offer: "Carry your bags, Boss?" (Jastrow 1913, 345)

Although Joseph Jastrow was not trained abroad, his father, brother, and other relatives held degrees from European universities. Perhaps for that reason he remained keenly informed of the history and patterns of university structures, curricula, and administrations worldwide. It was in the context of such a heightened sensitivity and understanding that, within the span of just the first decade or two of his career, he experienced the period of the most rapid change in structure of American institutions of higher education, changes that brought us the American university as we know it today. Along with a band of courageous colleagues, he was heroically vocal in raising the alarm at many of those changes—especially the sudden rise of what he perceived as the new, bizarre, and wholly American phenomenon of the university or college president, which stood out, he argued, as completely at odds with the democratic ideals of the society.

Jastrow gives us a chronology of the aggrandizement of the office. The new presidents appear, in many cases, no longer as kindred spirits in the community of scholars. Many colleges become feudal fiefdoms with the president as lord of the manor. The phenomenon of the lavish inauguration of new presidents makes its appearance—perhaps the term "coronation" better fits Jastrow's description. But it was the backgrounds and orientation of this new breed of administrator, much more than any ceremonial display, that presented by far the greater threat as Jastrow saw it: the new American university, now under their command, was to be run like an efficient retail business, and it was increasingly judged in terms of how well it responded to the immediate needs of the local but nonetheless external community— a criterion that, in Jastrow's view, ran altogether counter to the classic ideal of a university.

Along with the many briefer editorials he published in the popular press making known these perceptions were the following more developed statements:

- 1905. Invited address at inauguration of President James, University of Illinois.
- 1906. The academic career. Science Vol. 23.
- 1908. Address at 75th anniversary of Oberlin College.
- 1908. Academic aspects of administration. Popular Science Monthly Vol. 73.
- 1912. The administrative peril in education. Popular Science Monthly Vol. 77.
- 1913. The administrative peril in education. Expanded version. *In* University Control, J. M. Cattell, Ed. Columbia University Press. New York.

In all these statements, Jastrow frequently quotes from "editorials" in several popular magazines, citing no author. Some checking reveals that he was himself the author of the editorials he cites. There is much redundancy and repetition in these statements. The force of his critique, however, increases sequentially through those statements and culminates in the final and longest of them. Most of the following summary will in fact be drawn from that 1913 paper unless otherwise noted. The 1913 paper is worth summarizing if only because it is now a rare item found in few libraries. It is in this paper that Jastrow crosses over the line for the first time to find merit in his more radical colleagues' argument for the abolition of the American university presidency. His more consistent position had been that this officer should be hired and controlled solely by the faculty and that the duties and powers of the office be controlled by the faculty. As Jastrow tells it, such control had been taken away from most American faculties at about the same time it was returned to faculties in despotic czarist Russia. He was also fond of arguing that in the country of his origins, Germany, widely regarded as an authoritarian society, no educational administrative officer as despotic as the American university presidency would have been tolerated.

It is worth noting here that several of the new professors of psychology in American universities were in the forefront of this battle. Cattell, at Columbia, is still known today for the warnings he sounded at the same time as Jastrow's. In fact, they worked closely together, coordinating their protests. Cattell's position, however, was complicated by his related involvement in antiwar endeavors and by accusations against him of abuses of professorial authority. Two other pioneer psychologists who joined Jastrow in this crusade were George M. Stratton at the University of California and George Trumbull Ladd at Yale, both of whom Jastrow frequently quotes. Evidence is clear in some cases and strongly suggestive in others that the careers of these men were severely inhibited as a result of this activity. These men and some sympathetic colleagues from other disciplines had constituted the left wing of the group who created the American Association of University Professors, which, unfortunately for them, was not able to achieve the goal of recovering control of the universities from the new class of external administrators.

What had happened at the turn of the century in American higher education, as Jastrow saw it, that led to such controversy, at the center of which Jastrow held forth with the most acid of pens and tongues? It was, to be sure, an aspect of the phenomenon of American supergrowth and expansion in a climate in which the values of a business culture were taken for a model. When Jastrow arrived at the 700-student University of Wisconsin, its president, T. C. Chamberlin, was a fellow scientist, scholar, and teacher, a like-spirited academic colleague of equal socioeconomic status with his faculty. Presidents were sought because they were great teachers, and one of their foremost functions was to teach. Before Chamberlin, we find in John Bascom, a professor from Williams College and another teacher-administrator, a scholar with enough dedication to academic concerns to have interested Jastrow's teacher G. Stanley Hall in psychology. And Hall later preserved the image of the scholar-president when he presided at Clark University.

The social life on the Wisconsin campus was found in its young men's literary clubs, whose meetings the president himself might often attend. Life was simple, even primitive in physical accommodations, yet it constantly celebrated the arts, sciences, history, literature, and languages.

Then things began to explode in all directions as the nation's population erupted and new demands, stemming from surging American cultural trends, were made on the university, as Jastrow (1913) recounted. It was necessary, as he readily conceded, to bring in a new breed of president, in fact a "management" person, who could oversee the expansion of real estate, buildings, and programs, that radically changing conditions made necessary. The need of such changes was making itself felt early on at Cornell, where Charles Adams was president, the man who had denied Jastrow a position there. Leaving a storm of controversy behind him at Cornell, Adams accepted in 1892 a new and more powerfully defined presidency at, of all places, Jastrow's University of Wisconsin.

Such new-era administrators attracted new attention and new interests to the universities as their institutions expanded rapidly in new directions. These booster presidents imposed their externally approved business values. In that process, with things happening so rapidly, something of a coup took place before the less-practical academic mind could digest it and react. The university now approximated more literally than ever before the American corporate model, or in Jastrow's words, the model of the department store or the factory. The new type of president, as a businessman or banker usually external to the community of scholars, was brought in by an equally external board of trustees with little knowledge of the educational and cultural functions and traditions of the university. Jastrow (1913, 332) argued that

... bookkeeping in terms of intellectual and spiritual incomes is so difficult; values of ideals are so subject to difference of appraisal by shifting standards, that university authorities are sorely tempted to abandon the attempt, and put their investments in real estate—buildings, plants, and inventories of trade catalogues—to be pointed at with pride so long as one is blessed with an easy conscience.

And as well, the new administrators found themselves in positions of absolute power over their institutions. This meant they could dictate what music should be played and what not played, what poetry could and could not be read, what sort of science taught, and so on, though they themselves were often not educated in those fields.

Of course Jastrow acknowledged several distinguished and established American schools to which this portrait did not apply. He was talking, however, about the mainstream, the growing majority of aggressively new or rebuilding American colleges and universities in which a newly powerful president could refer to his faculty hirelings as "my boys" and offer them as various forms of entertainment to local communities. Relations between faculty and president changed radically as the new power structure emerged. Jastrow recalled, "It is within my experience to have professors summoned inquisitorially before a committee of the board to give an account of themselves, the interview conducted by the chairman with his feet on the table, and displaying a salivary agility that needs no further description" (1913, 345).

The growth of the expanding schools fed on itself, as Jastrow notes, to emerge in the form of cutthroat competition for students, offering them various inducements and entertainments. Growth in itself then eventually became an independent goal, as in the nation's greater economy in general. The university now often designated the local community as a target of public-relations activity in the interest of developing new support for its ever-increasing needs. Campuses were becoming architecturally extravagant. At Wisconsin, Adams abolished the literary clubs and introduced the Greek fraternity system in their place. College from now on was to be more fun. He then assembled a large town meeting of Madison citizenry to announce his proposal to introduce the new sport of American football, through which the university could enliven the life of the local community (cited in Levin 1963). The age of the building of the giant football stadium was about to unfold.

Standing in the background, and eventually lost in the crowd, stood the forlorn Joseph Jastrow, surely with eyes wide and mouth agape. For in these and many other sudden changes, the faculty had not been consulted. In many places they had lost control completely.

New colleges were being founded rapidly as the public responded positively to the new inducements of the renewed American university and college image. Jastrow refers to the "superfluous ease with which colleges and universities have been sprinkled over the land, and the misguided zeal of local ambition, and the passion for quick returns" (1913, 344). The faculties in those new schools often never had power to begin with, and so may have had less of a sense of what had been lost. But they were all keenly aware, as Jastrow notes in delicious detail, of the new hordes of improperly motivated and poorly prepared students lacking any intellectual interests. For now they were sorely in need of customers, tuition-payers, for this expanding business enterprise.

When Jastrow began his polemical assaults, he thereafter never received an increase in salary at Wisconsin (a period of approximately thirty years). Because of the expenses he had incurred in building his palace of culture in Madison, he was driven into bankruptcy. He remained in debt for years to his father and to his wife's relatives who had bailed him out.

Reforms did eventually occur, in a spotty way as we know. The tenure system was instituted. The new university management teams became better skilled at bringing in their faculty employees as members of the management team. The new management grew more polished, more diplomatic, an approach which in Jastrow's opinion was more insidious than the early feet-on-the-table spitting style, cited above. In a survey of the nation's faculties taken by Cattell, cited in Jastrow 1913, the majority (72%) of faculty continued to oppose the externalized administrative structure of the university as it emerged in the early twentieth century. But as Jastrow also concluded, the large majority of those faculty were too timid to protest out of fear for their own security. More and more they found ways to conform to the system, even to play it to their own advantage. In Jastrow's eyes this conformity was producing a race of academic sycophants, competing with each other for favors from the intimidating, though nonscholarly, administrators now residing in the most resplendent buildings on the highest hills on the campuses, and commanding the salaries of corporate executives. Yet ironically, as the corporate model took firmer hold of the university, the faculty, in Jastrow's analysis, became less and less of a corporate whole. The new administrations had the effect of subdividing the community of scholars into increasingly competitive factions, and the corporate model was extended down to the departmental level.

Jastrow imagined that most, if not all American colleges, were, as a result of these changes, the laughingstock of the European academic community. He claimed that by 1913 he could sense a resultant decline in the quality and character of individuals choosing the academic profession in this country. It was about at this time that the American entertainment media's stereotype of the professor as an absent-minded and silly fool gained wide credence. Universities began to teach through the edifice of their own structures, as Jastrow says, "that discovering truth and imparting the vital principle whereby others may discover it are of a dignity less than that of organizing and management" (1913, 325).

When Jastrow's wife Rachel died in 1925, he had already been for some time gravely dispirited about the academic profession and his situation in it. He then resigned his professorship and left for the East to take up a career as a professional writer and columnist. He was for two years a lecturer at the New School for Social Research in New York. The spectre of antisemitism animating the Wisconsin administration may have lurked behind some of his rude treatment there. While this is entirely in the realm of hearsay, and came to me as oral history, it did appear to have been confirmed by several independent sources at the Wisconsin psychology centenary in 1988, a case in point being Jastrow's replacement, the young Harry Israel, a brilliant young experimental and comparative psychologist from Stanford. Before Israel could sign his contract at Wisconsin, he had to be persuaded to hide his Jewish-sounding name, and he was thus induced to change his name to "Harlow."

Jastrow could not have foreseen the course that academic history would take through to the end of the century, the adjustments that have been made, nor the progressive refinement of the corporate model as applied to American higher education. As far as I know, he did not comment on the increase in the quality of faculty won by America as a result of the exodus from Hitler's Europe. He lingered on in poor health in the East, eventually died alone, having finally no heirs, no close relatives, and no close friends nearby. He had spent his last year in treatment for clinical depression at the Austen Riggs Foundation in Massachusetts in 1944. Jastrow had made one statement in the midst of his sounding of alarms early in the century that suggests he would remain quite as unimpressed with today's mega-universities as he was with their progenitors:

It would undoubtedly be the most beneficial fate that could happen to many of our universities to-day, if for a considerable period they built no new buildings, added no new departments, found their enrollment gradually decreasing and centered all their energies upon the internal elevation of true university ends, upon providing, for student and professor alike, the intellectual environment in which those interest thrive, for which student and professor come together, by which the academic ideal is inspired. (Jastrow 1906, 571)

REFERENCES

DUNLAP, K. 1907. Review of *The Subconscious* by J. Jastrow. Science **22**: 848–849.
JASTROW, J. 1906. The academic career as affected by administration. Science **23**: 561–574.
JASTROW, J. 1913. The administrative peril in education. *In* University Control. J. M. Cattell, Ed. Columbia University Press. New York.
JASTROW, J. 1928. Watson's behaviorism. The Saturday Review **5**: 28–30.
JASTROW, J. 1935. Has psychology failed? Am. Scholar **4**: 261–269.
KIMBLE, G. A., M. WERTHEIMER & C. L. WHITE., Eds. 1991. Portraits of Pioneers in Psychology. Erlbaum Associates. Hillsdale, NJ.
LEVIN, A. L. 1963. The Jastrows in Madison: A chronicle of university life, 1888–1900. Wisconsin Magazine of History. Vol. 64, Summer.

Christine Ladd-Franklin's Color Theory: Strategy for Claiming Scientific Authority?

LAUREL FURUMOTO

Department of Psychology
Wellesley College
Wellesley, Massachusetts 02181

In the 1891–1892 academic year, Christine Ladd-Franklin and her husband Fabian Franklin, accompanied by their 7-year-old daughter Margaret, traveled to Germany for Fabian's sabbatical. Fabian and Christine had met at Johns Hopkins University where he was a faculty member in mathematics and she was a student in mathematics and logic from 1878 through 1882. Their romance blossomed in the spring of Christine's last year at Johns Hopkins and they married in August 1882. The following summer Christine gave birth to a son who lived only a few days. The summer after that Margaret was born, a daughter who was the apple of her parents' eyes.

An avid science student from her undergraduate years at Vassar in the 1860s where she was inspired by her astronomy professor, Maria Mitchell, Christine Ladd-Franklin turned her attention in the 1880s to the topic of vision. In an account written when she was in her eighties, Ladd-Franklin (1928) recalled that her "interest in the theory of vision began with her investigation (in 1886) of the nature of the horopter, a mathematical question concerning binocular vision" (p. 139). In 1887 her paper on the horopter was published in the first number of the *American Journal of Psychology*.

During the first half of Fabian's sabbatical year in Germany Christine was able to study color vision in G. E. Müller's laboratory in Göttingen and during the second half to work in Berlin in Helmholtz's laboratory with Arthur König, a physicist interested in color vision. Reflecting more than 30 years later on that time in Germany, Ladd-Franklin (1928) observed:

> The combination of these experiences had a most interesting consequence. Professor Müller, at Göttingen, was a disciple of Hering, and an ardent supporter of Hering's theory of color-vision; Professor König, at Berlin, was equally devoted to the theory of his illustrious chief, Helmholtz. In the scientific world at large, opinion was divided between these two utterly diverse explanations of the phenomena of color-vision, each of which took account of one-half of the facts of color and wholly ignored the other half. (p. 139)

She recalled that in the midst of writing an article to show that a theory proposed by Donders was better than that of Helmholtz or Hering "it suddenly dawned upon her that a far better theory still was possible" (p. 139). This improved theory was capable of taking "full account of both the sets of facts" explained by the Hering and the Helmholtz theories and did so by taking into consideration "the course of development of the color sense," a factor "ignored by the adherents of both the rival theories" (p. 139).

At the time of her discovery, she wrote excitedly to Fabian, who was in Göttingen engaged in mathematical studies and looking after seven-year-old Margaret while Christine carried out research with König in Berlin. She told him that although her new theory had been created only last Sunday, she had to have it written up by the following Sunday:

> German, diagrams, and all,—in order to secure *priority,* and König says he has long been expecting at any moment to see the definitive theory appear every time he takes up a journal. . . . This haste is all his idea. He does not know my theory yet, only I have told him it is good. Isn't he sweet?

Christine's letter to Fabian bears the date July 7, 1892. It appears that he was not the only one to whom she communicated the news of her theoretical breakthrough, for in a letter dated July 16, 1892, G. F. Stout, the editor of *Mind,* wrote to her insisting that some account of her new theory of color vision ought to appear in his journal. If she were not prepared to give him an article, Stout (1892) said he should "at least expect a note on the subject giving the salient points of the new theory." And he went on to promise her "I shall do my utmost to procure a thorough discussion of your views in *Mind.*"

Stout may also have been instrumental in arranging for what turned out to be Ladd-Franklin's first public announcement of her theory the following month in a paper which she read at the International Congress of Psychology in London. In his letter he inquired whether she was planning to attend the Congress and suggested that reading a paper there on color vision would be "a good way of bringing your new theory before the world." Stout observed that it might still be possible to add her to the program and asked Ladd-Franklin's permission to consult with either Henry Sidgwick, president of the upcoming Congress, or James Sully, one of the honorary secretaries, about this.

An abstract of the paper that Ladd-Franklin delivered was distributed at the Congress of Experimental Psychology in London on August 2, 1892, and the full paper titled "A New Theory of Light-Sensation" appeared in the proceedings of the Congress published later the same year. Thus 1992 marks the centennial of the creation, the announcement, and the publication of the Ladd-Franklin theory of color vision.

Christine Ladd-Franklin was to spend the remainder of her life—nearly four decades—promoting her theory. Although she never held a regular academic appointment, she occasionally offered courses on color vision (and also on logic) at Johns Hopkins between 1904 and 1909 and at Columbia University in the teens and the twenties after Fabian accepted a position that moved the family to New York City in 1909. In 1912 and again in 1913 she gave a series of three lectures on color theory under the sponsorship of the department of psychology to audiences at Columbia University. In 1913, she repeated her lecture series at Clark and at Harvard University, and in 1914, at the University of Chicago.

In the decade that followed the creation of her color theory, Ladd-Franklin published prolifically on the topic of vision in *Science, Mind, Nature,* and the *Psychological Review.* A list of her publications includes 36 contributions to the literature, mostly in the area of color vision, from 1893 to 1902 (Murchison 1932). During this decade, Ladd-Franklin was also an associate editor and contributor on the topic of vision for the second volume of the *Dictionary of Philosophy and Psychology* (Baldwin 1902). She continued to publish in the area of vision and to attend psychological meetings to present her theoretical ideas both in the United States and abroad until her death in 1930.

Here and there over the years in her voluminous correspondence with psychologists, physicists, and physiologists interested in color vision, scattered references indicate that Ladd-Franklin had long been considering writing a book on the topic. For reasons that are not entirely clear, the projected definitive work was never realized. Instead, in the late twenties, Ladd-Franklin arranged to bring out a collection of her articles on color vision published between 1892 and 1926. The volume appeared in 1929 as part of a series: the *International Library of Psychology Philosophy and Scientific Method.* The general editor for the series, C. K. Ogden, wrote a preface to the book in which he proffered an explanation for Ladd-Franklin's decision to publish a collection of reprinted work instead of the original volume she had long contemplated:

> Dr. Ladd-Franklin has written, in the course of a long and belligerent career, many vigorous articles on the subject of colour vision; she maintains that she could not do half as well again if she were to write afresh all the matter that they contain. (p. vii)

Ogden went on to inform the reader that it had been decided, therefore, to bring the articles out "as they stand, with indications in square brackets (chiefly footnotes) where emendations were required" (p. vii).

The topic of the book. as Ogden noted in his preface, is the Ladd-Franklin theory of color. The purpose of the book and of Ladd-Franklin's tireless promotion of her theory over the course of several decades can be viewed as something quite different, namely, a strategy that Ladd-Franklin used to claim scientific authority. In the remainder of this paper I will first provide the reader with a brief description of Ladd-Franklin's theory as it is presented in her book and then go on to discuss the grounds for viewing it as a vehicle that Ladd-Franklin used in attempting to secure herself a place in science.

Ladd-Franklin took great pains to have included in her book a series of colored charts that illustrated her theory of color sensation. Although she referred to the charts as a "kindergarten method of enabling one to hold in mind all at once the curiously complicated (apparently contradictory) phenomena of color," she obviously regarded them as an indispensable aid to comprehending the vast and bewildering array of facts about color vision.

Her first chart illustrated "the fundamental fact insisted upon by Hering . . . that, as light sensation vision is tetrachromatic—there are *four* chromatic sensations": yellow, blue, red, and green (p. 275). Captioned "First Crude Analysis of the Colour Sense" the chart reinforced Ladd-Franklin's assertion that "he spectrum (and the world) is made up of four chromatic 'elements'" plus white, an achromatic color sensation (p. 276).

Turning next to the major rival of the Hering theory, Ladd-Franklin observed: "The Helmholtz theory is commonly said to be a 'trichromatic' theory, but this is to use the word *chromatic* in a totally wrong sense; what Helmholtz maintained . . . is that three specific light frequencies" are sufficient "when mixed, to reproduce the whole gamut of color" (p. 275). This fact was represented in Ladd-Franklin's second chart by a diagram of three experimental curves "based upon most painstaking work done in the laboratory of Helmholtz" by Arthur König showing the proportion of each of the three specific light frequencies required to match colors throughout the spectrum. The "König–Helmholtz analysis," Ladd-Franklin insisted, "should be expressed by saying that light-sensation begins with an *initial trireceptor process*" and has "nothing to say about the number of sensation elements experienced."

The Hering "fact" that our experience of color is tetrachromatic and the Helmholtz "fact" that three physical constituents are sufficient to produce all experienced colors, Ladd-Franklin noted, have "wrongly been assumed to be contradictory" (p. 275). Challenging this view, Ladd-Franklin asserted, "they are both, when rightly considered, absolutely true." Both of "these two fundamental facts," which Ladd-Franklin thought of as pertaining to different stages of the visual process, were folded into her theory. She referred to them as constituting "two of its three fundamental building stones" (p. 276). The third foundational element, which she viewed as her original contribution, was the idea of the evolutionary development of the color sense. Ladd-Franklin elaborated this conceptualization in two other of her charts—one a representation of the evolution of the color sense, the other a diagram of a hypothetical molecule mediating fully evolved color vision.

Presenting her theory of how the color sense evolved, Ladd-Franklin wrote:

In Carboniferous times, when there were no coloured birds and no coloured flowers, a colour-sense would have been of no use to the low animals which existed—their vision was achromatic. (That of the cat and of other night-prowling animals is achromatic still.) In the Cretaceous period came in together bees and coloured flowers. But the bees . . . see two colours only (yellow and blue) like . . . partially colour-blind individuals, their vision is dichromatic. With birds, most mammals, and normal human beings, yellow has been differentiated into red and green—vision has become tetrachromatic." (p. 280)

The other chart depicted what Ladd-Franklin called "the assumed co-lour-molecule," a hypothetical light-sensitive molecule that mediated fully evolved color vision. She described her theory about how it produced color sensations in the following way: "Under the influence of *specific* light-rays" the molecule underwent "partial dissociation" (p. 277). According to Ladd-Franklin:

When green light and blue light strike it together, the dual colour-blends (the green-blues) are experienced; under the influence of red light and blue light together the red-blues (the purples) occur; but when red light and green light fall together upon the retina, what happens? Instead of our seeing the red-greens, these two nerve-excitants at once unite chemically into the *yellow* nerve-excitant out of which they were differentiated, and what we see is yellow. (p. 277)

This concludes the brief exposition of the substance of the Ladd-Franklin theory of color vision. Next, we will look at evidence suggesting that Ladd-Franklin's lifelong dedication to promoting her theory was a strategy for claiming scientific authority.

To begin, it is important to realize that Ladd-Franklin was trying to forge a career as a scientist in an era when to do so was a rarity for women. Born in 1847, she grew up during a period when the doctrine of separate spheres for men and women was in full force. This doctrine prescribed a clear division between men's work and women's work, with women's lying in the private domestic realm and men's lying outside in the public arena. What this meant for nineteenth-century white, middle-class women at whom the prescription of separate spheres was primarily directed, was that they were defined by their family life and their activities were determined in accordance with numerous claims that relatives had on them (Kerber 1988).

Women's identity was thus firmly rooted in and closely circumscribed by the family, while science during the nineteenth century was moving out of the domestic, amateur context into the public, professionalized arena. Pnina Abir-Am and Dorinda Outram (1987), editors of a volume examining women's participation in science over the past two centuries, maintain that early in the nineteenth century the production of science was still heavily dependent upon the help of family members and private patrons and the situation of men and women engaged in scientific pursuits was in many respects comparable. By 1900, they say that this was no longer true and women who aspired to scientific work suffered a clear disadvantage.

Case studies of women scientists included in their book reveal that these women encountered great obstacles and profound difficulties in gaining and exercising scientific authority. Because of their gender, they were subjected to a pattern of intense social and intellectual marginalization. Even the most talented women experienced constraints on their integration into main-stream science—which Abir-Am and Outram characterize as disciplinary and empiricist science.

What exceptions there were to this pattern of marginalization occurred usually as a result of a woman's special relationship with a male mentor who was able to pave the way for his female collaborator's integration into mainstream science. As for the other women, Abir-Am and Outram see them as "compelled to resort to transdisciplinary and theoretical strategies of claiming scientific authority" (p. 9) which nevertheless, they conclude, re-mained largely elusive.

Abir-Am and Outram's analysis aptly characterizes Ladd-Franklin's ca-reer in science. Born into an established New England family of some means and distinction, Kitty Ladd was heir to many enabling factors that helped mitigate the larger societal forces working against her entry into science. These include a mother and maternal aunts who were women's rights advo-cates; a concerned and supportive father; a professor and mentor—the Vassar astronomer Maria Mitchell—who provided a role model; and mar-riage to a fellow academic, Fabian Franklin, who encouraged and supported her work (Furumoto 1992).

Despite these countervailing forces and Ladd-Franklin's undisputed am-bition and intellectual brilliance, she confronted unyielding, gender-linked impediments to realizing a career in scientific psychology commensurate with her potential. Notable among these were the lack of a regular academic post, in an era when most psychologists were employed in colleges and universities, and exclusion from the meetings of a group considered by many to represent psychology's scientific elite.

Her inability to secure a regular academic position was a predictable consequence, in that time period, of her decision to marry. Highly educated women in the late nineteenth and early twentieth centuries were faced with what was termed "the cruel choice," the necessity to choose between the careers for which they had trained or marriage and a life of domesticity (Scarborough and Furumoto 1987). In deciding to marry Fabian Franklin, Ladd-Franklin effectively disqualified herself for the academic jobs that as a woman she might realistically have aspired to in that era, a position in a college for women or in a teachers college.

Another hindrance to advancing her career in scientific psychology imposed by her gender was exclusion from the elite society founded by Cornell's E. B. Titchener, "the Experimentalists" (Furumoto 1988). Titchener's group began meeting yearly in 1904, putting established experimental psychologists in contact with promising junior faculty and advanced graduate students.

Members of the society, primarily from elite Eastern universities, benefited by becoming part of an important communication network made up of a select group of newcomers to the field and in Titchener's own words, "the men who have arrived" (Furumoto 1988, 94). At the annual spring meetings held on campuses in the East, collegial relationships were fostered, and knowledge about laboratory apparatus, experimental techniques, and the latest research findings was shared. By Titchener's decree, and with the acquiescence of the other members, certain psychologists were excluded from these meetings, most notably women and those not considered experimentalists.

Thus in 1912, when Ladd-Franklin, who had been in correspondence with Titchener from the time he arrived at Cornell in 1892, wrote to say that she had a paper that she would very much like to read at his upcoming meeting, Titchener refused her request to attend. Ladd-Franklin, clearly indignant, replied, "I am shocked to know that you are still—at this year— excluding women from your meeting of experimental psychologists. It is such a very old-fashioned standpoint!" (Furumoto 1988, 107).

As old-fashioned and discriminatory a standpoint as Titchener may have represented, and in spite of the verbal abuse that Ladd-Franklin peppered him with two years later in 1914, calling his policy "so unconscientious, so immoral,—worse than that—so unscientific!" Titchener was unyielding. He again refused to let her attend a meeting of the Experimentalists to be held at Columbia University, as Ladd-Franklin exclaimed, "in New York—at my very door" (Furumoto 1988, 107). Titchener maintained his policy of not admitting women to the meetings of his society up until his death in 1927, and after hesitating for two years the new leadership of the group decided in 1929 to remove the "restriction of membership with regard to sex" (Furumoto 1988, 108).

As early as her undergraduate years at Vassar in the 1860s, Ladd-Franklin was aware of the constraints on women's participation in experimental science. Reflecting on this period of her life, she recalled that her "keenest interest at college" was "in physics," a subject she would have devoted herself to after graduation "had it not been for the impossibility, in those days, in the case of women, of obtaining access to laboratory facilities" (Ladd-Franklin 1928, 136). She reports taking up "as the next best subject, mathematics, which could be carried on without any apparatus."

By 1891, when she and Fabian spent the year in Germany, Ladd-Franklin was admitted both to Müller's laboratory in Göttingen and that of Helmholtz in Berlin. As wryly noted by a leading authority on the history of women scientists in America, although at that time the professors in Germany were adamantly opposed to admitting women from their own country to the universities "foreign women were far less of a threat, since they would return home and not expect to teach in Germany" (Rossiter 1982, 43).

The product of Ladd-Franklin's sojourn in the German laboratories was her theory of color vision, a theory which she defended with all of her formidable intellectual and logical powers for the rest of her life. The capstone of this effort is clearly her book, *Colour and Colour Theories* (1929) where her writing on the topic over the years is collected between two covers. What a careful reading of this work reveals is that it is more than simply a collection of papers. Ladd-Franklin used the "emendations that the work required," in the words of her editor in his preface to the work, for a very specific purpose. These "emendations" consisted chiefly of lengthy, added footnotes in which Ladd-Franklin attempted to set the record straight about her empirical contributions to the psychology of vision. More specifically, they highlight the fact that in her eyes these contributions had not been properly acknowledged by certain male researchers.

A reading of her footnotes reveals that she bore grudges against two individuals in particular—Herman Ebbinghaus and Arthur König—because each took credit for experimental findings that she claimed as her own. In the case of Ebbinghaus, priority was the issue, as Ladd-Franklin made clear in a footnote almost a page long:

> Professor Ebbinghaus has never explained how it happened that he published his "discovery" of the extension of the Purkinje phenomenon to colourless light without any reference to my previous announcement of the same fact. He could not easily have been unaware of it, for his experiments were carried out in the same laboratory as mine—Professor König's—and he listened to my paper read before the Psychological Congress at London (1892) of which a printed abstract was also distributed. Professor Ebbinghaus was, not unnaturally, very angry with me when my note on this subject came out in Nature (1893) and for 15 years

we were not on speaking terms; finally however, through the kind offices of Prof. Deussen at the end of the International Congress of Psychology at Heidelberg (1908) we became reconciled. (pp. 195–196)

With König her complaint was that he gave her less credit than she deserved for a discovery she made while working in his laboratory. Ladd-Franklin returned to Germany on her own in 1894 to spend the summer doing research with König in Berlin. Initially she was ecstatic about the laboratory work she was doing in the letters she wrote to Fabian who, back in Baltimore, aided by family members, was looking after 10-year-old Margaret. However, as the summer wore on, Ladd-Franklin became more and more reticent about discussing her work and doubtful about the outcome of her labors. By August, she was clearly disheartened. She wrote to Fabian accusing König "of stepping into her field" and of not giving her sufficient recognition for her "little discovery of the absence of adaptation in the fovea," adding in exasperation, "but what can one expect from a man!" (Ladd-Franklin 1894).

Ladd-Franklin waited more than 30 years before making public her accusation of König in print. Her book contains a paper originally published in 1895 in which she reported some research that she had done while in König's laboratory. In 1927, she added the following footnote to it:

In this 1895 paper I gave a detailed account of the circumstances attending my discovery of the "normal night blindness of the fovea." This way by way of claiming priority for a discovery for which König was by this time not giving me sufficient credit—in fact, none at all. (p. 92)

She went on to remark mordantly: "Von Kries even now attributes this discovery to König *und seine Genossen.*" *Genossen* is a masculine noun in German, and the phrase can be translated into English as "König and his (male) cronies."

With these unhappy memories from the 1890s that attended her forays into laboratory and empirical work, it is plausible to imagine Ladd-Franklin deciding to focus her logical mind and her energy on theory as an alternative route to scientific authority. It was an endeavor that absorbed her for the rest of her life. However, in common with most of the other talented women scientists of her day, the sought-for authority largely evaded her grasp.

As Ogden observed in his preface to Ladd-Franklin's book: "It is one of the minor misfortunes of science that the Ladd-Franklin theory of the colour-sensations should have been so long in securing recognition" (p. viii). And if one were to inquire about the staying power of that recognition, by consulting contemporary textbooks that discuss theories of color vision, one would discover yet another misfortune. For typically in these works, the predecessors of the Ladd-Franklin theory—the rival theories of Hering and Helmholtz—remain preserved as part of the landscape of the past, while Ladd-Franklin's has vanished from the scene.

REFERENCES

ABIR-AM, P. G. & D. OUTRAM., Eds. 1987. Uneasy Careers and Intimate Lives: Women in Science 1789–1979. Rutgers University Press. New Brunswick, NJ.

BALDWIN, J. M., Ed. 1902. Dictionary of Philosophy and Psychology, Vol. 2. Macmillan. New York.

FURUMOTO, L. 1988. Shared knowledge: The Experimentalists, 1904–1929. *In* The Rise of Experimentation in American Psychology. J. G. Morawski, Ed.: 94–113. Yale University Press. New Have, CT.

FURUMOTO, L. 1992. Joining separate spheres—Christine Ladd-Franklin, woman-scientist (1847–1930). Am. Psychologist **47**: 175–182.

KERBER, L. K. 1988. Separate spheres, female worlds, woman's place: The rhetoric of women's history. J. Am. Hist. **75**: 9–39.

LADD-FRANKLIN, C. 1887. The experimental determination of the horopter. Am. J. Psychol. 1 99–111.

LADD-FRANKLIN, C. 1892, to F. Franklin, July 7. The Christine Ladd-Franklin and Fabian Franklin Papers, Rare Book and Manuscript Library. Columbia University. New York.

LADD-FRANKLIN, C. 1892. A new theory of light sensation. Proc. Int. Cong. Exper. Psychol. London.

LADD-FRANKLIN, C. 1894, to F. Franklin, Aug. 10. The Christine Ladd-Franklin and Fabian Franklin Papers, Rare Book and Manuscript Library. Columbia University. New York.

LADD-FRANKLIN, C. 1928. the Biographical Cyclopedia of American Women. Vol. **3**: 135–141. Williams-Wiley. New York.

LADD-FRANKLIN, C. 1929. Colour and Colour Theories. Kegan Paul. London.

MURCHISON, C. 1932. The Psychological Register. Vol. **3**: 290–291. Clark University Press. Worcester, MA.

ROSSITER, M. W. 1982. Women Scientists in America: Struggles and Strategies to 1940. The Johns Hopkins University Press. Baltimore, MD.

SCARBOROUGH, E., & L. FURUMOTO. 1987. Untold Lives: The First Generation of American Women Psychologists. Columbia University Press. New York.

STOUT, G. F.,1892, to C. Ladd-Franklin, July 16. The Christine Ladd-Franklin and Fabian Franklin Papers, Rare Book and Manuscript Library. Columbia University. New York.

Recognition for Women: The Problem of Linkage

ELIZABETH SCARBOROUGH

Indiana University South Bend
South Bend, Indiana 46634

A 1992 book review in *Contemporary Psychology* begins with the assertion that "every academic discipline has been affected by the recent scholarship on women and gender" (Muehlenhard 1992, 123). Though one might question such a sweeping generalization, certainly our understanding of psychology's history is being broadened because of current scholarship dealing with the history of women in science and in the professions. The titles of several works published within the last ten years or so convey the tenor of what is being considered: *Beyond Separate Spheres* (Rosenberg 1982), *Women Scientists in America: Struggles and Strategies to 1940* (Rossiter 1982), *Unequal Colleagues: The Entrance of Women into the Professions* (Glazer and Slater 1987), *Uneasy Careers and Intimate Lives* (Abir-Am and Outram 1987), *Untold Lives: The First Generation of American Women Psychologists* (Scarborough and Furumoto 1987), *Sexual Science, the Victorian Construction of Womanhood* (Russett 1989), *The Mind Has No Sex? Women in the Origins of Modern Science* (Schiebinger 1989), *Women of Science: Righting the Record* (Kass-Simon, Farnes, and Nash 1990), and most recently, *The Outer Circle: Women in the Scientific Community* (Zuckerman, Cole, and Bruer 1991).

Only one of those books focused exclusively on psychology, but the centennial celebration of the American Psychological Association (APA) has stimulated a number of publications that examine the women of psychology, with special emphasis on their status and participation in the history of the discipline and its organizations. Articles collected in a special issue of the *Psychology of Women Quarterly* (O'Connell and Russo 1991) are an excellent resource. Here I share some of my thinking about the women who have participated in psychology's century of achievement and puzzle a bit about why these women, many of whom were quite accomplished, have until just now received so little recognition. This is what I mean by the "problem of linkage"; it refers to the lack of correspondence between accomplishment and recognition.

First, I present a sketch of the APA's history with emphasis on the roles played by women, drawing from a chapter in the centennial volume edited by Rand Evans, Virginia Sexton, and Tom Cadwallader entitled *The American Psychological Association: A Historical Perspective* (Scarborough, 1992). Next I discuss findings related to how recognition is achieved in science and explanations for women's lower research productivity. Finally I conclude by considering how historians have dealt with women in psychology.

WOMEN IN THE APA

The APA's 100 years of history, when viewed from the women's perspective, seems most reasonably to divide into three periods: the first 30 years, the middle 50, and the last 20. As these periods are unequal in time span, they were also unequal in opportunities for women to function as full participants. The first 30 years, 1892–1921, were a time of growth for the APA and of eager entrance by women. This period, however, was followed by a full half century, 1922–1971, when women, though increasingly attracted to psychology, found their professional opportunities sharply limited and their status as professionals seriously questioned. In the last period, spanning the 1970s and 1980s, there are indications that women are moving toward parity in both opportunity and status. Let me now characterize those three periods in more detail.

1892–1921

During its first 30 years, 15% of the members admitted to the APA were women. (See Scarborough and Furumoto 1987 for a discussion of the first generation of women psychologists.) It is well known that no women were included in the first meetings when the APA was formed in 1892. However, James McKeen Cattell, a member of the APA's first Council, nominated both Mary Whiton Calkins and Christine Ladd-Franklin to membership, and they were elected in the second year, presumably on the basis of their having contributed to the literature through journal publications. Though neither of them held the Ph.D., each had undertaken doctoral-level study. Almost all of the women elected subsequently (72 of 77 by the year 1921) were degree holders; the proportion of members with the Ph.D. was higher for women than for men. The women's research fields included the full range of topics. Men and women held almost equal interests in the experimental area, but by 1920 women were more highly represented in applied and less in theoretical fields than were men (Fernberger 1928). Their degree status and identification with research are important factors, showing that the women had undergone the careful research training required to "do" psychology and were engaged in scientific work.

Women were active in presenting papers at APA meetings. Most of the papers dealt with experimental research (53%) or testing (29%). The women's inclusion in the governance structure was more limited. Several were appointed to ad hoc committees, and both Mary Calkins and Margaret Washburn served on the Council and were elected president. During its first 30 years, then, the APA welcomed women as members. These women contributed regularly to psychology's knowledge base, but only a handful received recognition by being included in leadership roles.

1922–1972

During the next 50 years, women continued to enter psychology and came to represent a third of the APA's membership. Despite their presence, however, women psychologists did not gain status and recognition proportional to their numbers, either in the field or in the APA. After Washburn's presidency, it was 50 years before the APA elected its next woman president.

Midway in this period, in 1946, the APA was reorganized to bring back into one organization the practitioners who in the 1930s had split off from the academically controlled APA to form the American Association for Applied Psychology (see Capshew and Hilgard 1992). By this time, women psychologists had become clustered in the applied fields and held a numerical advantage there. Following the reorganization, women figured more prominently in the "new" APA, though still not with parity in status and leadership roles. From 1947 through 1971 eight women were elected to the Board of Directors. The 1960s were a particularly bleak time, however. In three years of that decade, no woman served on the Board; for the other years, only a single woman was elected to serve. Another form of recognition was instituted in 1956 when the APA established an awards program, the first award being for distinguished scientific contributions. Only two women, Nancy Bayley and Eleanor J. Gibson, were among the 48 persons who received that honor prior to 1972.

1972–1991

The last 20 years have seen a dramatic shift in the way women have been recognized in the APA. In 1970 a task force was established to examine the status of women in psychology. This was followed by an ad hoc committee on the status of women, which became the continuing Committee on Women in Psychology. Earlier efforts to establish a division to address women's interests had been thwarted, but in 1973 the Division of the Psychology of Women was approved. In 1977 the Women's Program Office, now located in the Public Interest Directorate, was established. Increased recognition for individual women came also with their election to high office in the governance structure: five have served as president since 1972 (Anne Anastasi, Leona Tyler, Florence Denmark, Janet Spence, and Bonnie Strickland); one is currently serving as treasurer (Judith Albino); and fifteen have been elected to the Board of Directors. Other indicators, such as election to the Council of Representatives and to Fellow status, selection for participation through governance units, and receipt of outstanding awards, present a more ambiguous picture, but it is clear that women are receiving much more equitable recognition within the APA than was the case prior to 1971.

LINKAGE BETWEEN ACCOMPLISHMENT AND RECOGNITION

The topic of recognition for scientific work takes us into the social organization of science. My own thinking about the sociology of science has been influenced for some time by a work published by Warren Hagstrom (1965). Hagstrom used field research data from focused interviews conducted with faculty members in the "exact" sciences (mathematics, statistics, logic, physics, chemistry, biology, and metallurgy)—all men, as best I can tell. As Hagstrom portrays it, a social exchange model works powerfully in science, both as a means of social control and to regulate recognition. Manuscripts and presentations are "contributions"—gifts to one's colleagues in exchange for recognition of one's worth. Acceptance of the gift is acknowledged by its publication or an invitation to share it by addressing a scholarly gathering. Such acceptance signifies recognition for the donor and enhances one's status in the scholarly community. Thus, "the organization of science consists of an exchange" (Hagstrom 1965, 13), the exchange of information for social recognition. Gift-giving is what academics engage in at meetings such as this one sponsored by the New York Academy of Sciences!

In Hagstrom's view, it is "the desire to obtain recognition [that] induces scientists to publish their results" and thereby "to conform to scientific norms by contributing . . . discoveries to the larger community" (Hagstrom 1965, 16). Probably most would agree that publishing or "writing up results" is not in itself a gratifying activity. The intrinsically satisfying aspect of research is the discovery and synthesis of knowledge—the puzzle-solving aspect of science that functions as a strong motivator in historical scholarship also. So why do we publish? Because we value the recognition granted by our peers and because the gift exchange as a norm of science is part of our intense socialization in graduate school.

Institutional Recognition

Hagstrom delineated two forms of recognition: institutional and elementary. Institutionalized recognition is conferred in formal channels of communication, primarily through articles appearing in scientific journals, though papers read at public meetings may serve as substitutes for publication. Publication, and often paper presentation, follows acceptance by one's peers through the referee process and is thus an important form of recognition. A work considered really valuable, when received by a wider audience, will then be cited by later scholars—another form of recognition. Through publication and citation, then, one develops a reputation as a valued donor to the enterprise. Finally comes the collective institutionalized honor in the form of medals, prizes, awards, usually in ceremonial settings. As Hagstrom summarized the progression: "An individual establishes his status as a scientist by having his research contributions accepted by a reputable journal; he achieves prestige as a scientist by having his work cited and emulated by others; and he achieves elite status by receiving collective honors" (Hagstrom 1965, 28).

This scenario holds fairly well for psychology, where institutionalized recognition is typically conferred by election to high office in the APA as a collective honor, though one might argue that increasingly such recognition may depend on the office holder's ambition and political expertise as much as on his or her "donation" of knowledge to the field. And the use of the masculine pronoun in the quote just given is, for psychology, not simply a sexist anachronism. It does describe the situation for psychology as well as for science in general. Men publish more frequently than women, their works are cited more often, and they are much more likely to achieve elite status and exceptional honors (Helmreich et al. 1980; Helmreich and Spence 1982).

Elementary Recognition

Hagstrom is less clear in describing his second form of recognition, elementary recognition. Here he considers the informal situations in which interpersonal approval and esteem are given in return for information. These situations include personal contacts made at the large meetings of scientific societies, the smaller meetings of select groups (usually open only by invitation), and interaction between colleagues in research groups that may be geographically separated or located at the same institution or within one's university department.

Detailed data on how well such elementary recognition works for women in psychology are not now available. We do know that, early on, women were explicitly excluded from meetings of psychology's first informal organization of "insiders," the Society of Experimental Psychologists (Furumoto 1988; Scarborough and Furumoto 1987). My hunch is that for many, perhaps most, women today, both elementary and institutional recognition come to them in large part from their association with other women. One study reported that, in the fields of economics and psychology, men cite men and women cite women (Ferber 1986). Another (Cole 1979) asked sociologists, biologists, and psychologists to list people in their fields who were "leading contributors." Among the psychologists, 17 percent of the men named at least one woman, but 50 percent of the women named a woman. The pattern was almost identical for sociologists, but among biologists, men and women responded similarly, with 14 percent of the men and only 13 percent of the women mentioning another woman scientist. The APA's Division 35, Psychology of Women, has instituted an array of awards for women, but very few men attend the awards ceremony and probably very few see the newsletter in which the awards are announced. Certainly it is questionable whether women's separatist form of elementary recognition is an effective means for improving women's status in the larger arena.

Scientific Reputations

Hagstrom's work was done in the 1960s and did not consider gender issues. During the 1970s, however, with the rise of interest in gender differences, attention began to focus on comparative studies. An intriguing quantitative analysis by Jonathan Cole, reported in his book *Fair Science* (1979), examined the problem of sex discrimination by taking a hard look at inequities in science. Since recognition rests on one's scientific reputation, Cole's conclusions regarding reputation are pertinent to the problem of linkage for women. He dealt with a number of status sets such as the distinction of the scientist's institution and department, the academic rank held, the impact of research produced, and professional age. Here I can only report a few of Cole's findings. One is a significant interaction between gender, educational origin (i.e., the standing of the doctoral granting institution), and reputational standing. Men "can start off with greater institutional disadvantages than women and still make out fairly well" (Cole 1979, 139) provided they publish a lot of work and it is well received. Not so the women. As Cole put it, for women, "once they begin the race at a disadvantage, the race is pretty much run. The data suggest that a functional prerequisite for eventual prominence or esteem for the female scientist is to start out at a first-ranked institution" (Cole 1979, 139). Another interaction was found in the relationship between gender, chronological age, and reputational standing, to the definite disadvantage of older women. These and other items led Cole to identify different processes at work for women and men in achieving reputations and to suggest that "females are not as able as males to convert their performance into reputation, and that there may well be institutional impediments to this exchange" (p. 142).

Cole's conclusion that the process of reputation-building works differently for men and women was earlier labeled "the Woman Problem" by psychologist E. G. Boring. He detailed "standard operating procedures about the acquisition of prestige" (Boring 1961, 188) in psychology—a process very similar to that described by both Hagstrom and Cole. In Boring's view, "the Woman Problem exists because there is this competition and invidious comparison" (p. 192) and women are handicapped in the competition for prestige because of institutional barriers to their gaining administrative positions, their inherent greater interest in particular topics rather than broad generalities, their preference for working as practitioners, and their inability to engage in job-concentration ("professional fanaticism," p. 190) because of conflicts between career and family for women's commitment of time and energy.

The Triple Penalty

Harriet Zuckerman is another scholar who has been working in this field for some time. She and Cole have collaborated on a number of studies. In an early publication (Zuckerman and Cole 1975), they defined the "triple penalty" that women scientists have struggled to overcome in this century. As Cole later summarized it, "first, they had to overcome cultural barriers to their entering science and scholarly careers; second, after entering such careers, they had to overcome the widespread belief among scientists and scholars that they were either physiologically or psychologically incapable of creative work; and third, they had to overcome structural impediments to success—that is, actual discrimination in the allocation of opportunities and rewards within the academic community" (Cole 1979, 255). Biographical accounts of women psychologists support the notion that women psychologists have borne this triple penalty along with their sister scientists in other fields.

In a recent publication, Zuckerman reviews research that supports the conclusion that "women scientists' career attainments, on average, do not equal those of men" (Zuckerman 1991, 49). She goes on to consider various explanations, all related to the triple penalty, for the persistent gender inequalities. The explanations fall under four headings:

[1.] Gender differences in scientific ability
[2.] Gender differences arising from *social selection,* based on

(a) gender discrimination
(b) gender differences in role performance and the allocation of resources and rewards
[3.] Gender differences arising from *self-selection,* including
(a) marriage and motherhood and their consequences
(b) gender differences in career commitment
[4.] Outcomes of accumulation of advantage and disadvantage (Zuckerman 1991, 49).

She concludes that "the available evidence on each of these is ambiguous, not because the theories are unclear but because the data are complex, often vexingly incoherent, and frequently partial" (Zuckerman 1991, 49). Zuckerman ends by spelling out a research agenda, what we need to know and why, "domains of specified ignorance" to use Robert Merton's phrase.

Other chapters in the Zuckerman, Cole, and Bruer (1991) volume explore various aspects of the careers of women and men in science. Several examine research related to proposed explanations for the gender differences in publication productivity. Marriage and motherhood are associated with increased publication rates, rather than less as might be supposed and as E. G. Boring (1961) asserted. Detailed discussions focus on differential treatment of men and women in their work situations, differential socialization and aspirations, and prevailing cultural conceptions of scientific knowledge and gender. The obstacles encountered by women scientists are shown to be similar to those experienced by women other settings. Finally, Jonathan Cole and Burton Singer propose a "theory of limited differences" to describe how processes of self-selection, social selection, and cumulative advantage and disadvantage may help explain the productivity puzzle (i.e., differential rates for women and men). They demonstrate how even small differences, experienced early in the career by even a very small proportion, may compound to widen the gap over time, thereby accounting for the observation that older women scientists experience greater disparity in attainments.

HISTORIANS OF PSYCHOLOGY AND THE PROBLEM OF LINKAGE

I think no one can seriously argue these days that women are incapable of making valuable contributions to science, including psychological science, though there may yet be those who still believe (albeit privately) that women are generally less capable than men in science. An unbiased examination of psychology's history over the last century shows that women have proved themselves capable. They have entered psychology in impressive numbers and endured our socialization through doctoral level study. For a hundred years now, women have been at work doing research, producing knowledge and advancing psychology's base operations as well as producing and refining psychological theory. But the "exchange system" that should then have earned for them reciprocal recognition has worked only for a sharply limited few of these women. Many of the books cited at the beginning of this paper address, at least tangentially, the problem of linkage for women in science and the history of science. Indeed, a primary motivating factor in producing these works may be a strongly felt need to honor science's merito-cratic ideal—or note its failure—by "giving credit where credit is due."

That motive has stimulated a great deal of attention to the women in psychology's history (e.g., O'Connell and Russo 1983, 1988, and 1990), most though not all of this scholarship being conducted by women psychol-ogists themselves. It is clear now that, though in the aggregate women psychologists publish less and are cited less frequently than men and perhaps for that reason receive less institutional recognition, among psychology's women have been many exceptionally accomplished careerists. For them, the problem of linkage arises when we note that their contributions have not been adequately considered in our histories of psychology.

A study using both citation analysis and textbook coverage to evaluate the historical treatment of female psychologists (Eberts and Gray 1982) matched five of the early women (Christine Ladd-Franklin, Mary Whiton Calkins, Margaret Floy Washburn, June Etta Downey, and Leta Stetter Hollingworth) with five contemporary men (Edmund Clark Sanford, Ed-ward Wheeler Scripture, Walter Bowers Pillsbury, Walter Fenno Dearborn, and Warner Brown) to provide comparative data. On the citations count, using a statistical test, the men and women did not separate into different groups. This was true also for the textbook coverage measure, which used lines of text for rankings, although the test yielded considerable variability, with the range for the women being 2 to 12.5, for the men 2 to 391.5. More significantly, however, of the 20 textbooks used in the study (published between 1950 and 1976), nine made no mention of any of the five women.

A later examination of citations indicated that of the 25 first-generation women, 16 were still being cited in scientific journals between 1972 and 1984 (Scarborough and Furumoto 1987). Works by Margaret Washburn, Mary Calkins, and Kate Gordon, the most frequent publishers of the group, accounted for almost two-thirds of the citations. It appears that publishing psychologists have been fairer in their recognition of women's contributions than have been writers of textbook histories of psychology.

It might be argued that textbook writers are compilers, dependent on already published reviews of works and biographical studies, and that the invisibility of psychology's women until the surge of women's historiography in the 1970s and 1980s provided these writers with scant material on which to base discussions of women psychologists. Other explanations for the lack of attention to women in psychology's histories, some more invidious than others, have been suggested elsewhere (Scarborough and Furumoto 1987): a reliance on intellectual history with its accompanying emphasis on ideas and theories (where women are less well represented than in the applied aspects of the field), a presentist approach which disregards earlier work not now of interest, a filtering function occurring through compression of more material into smaller published packages, the obliteration phenomenon which makes invisible the originator of a widely used idea or technique, and covert devaluation of work done by women, be that work scientific or practical.

With increased attention being paid now in scholarly presentations to the contributions of women psychologists and with increased sensitivity to gender issues being widely espoused, we might hope that the problem of linkage will be addressed in historical writings, even as it appears to be decreasing in magnitude for today's women psychologists.

CONCLUSION

According to Zuckerman, although "there are *persisting differences* between men and women scientists on average, in role performance and career attainments when viewed cross-sectionally" and "these differences are almost always in the direction of comparative disadvantage for women . . . there are signs of *growing convergence* between men and women in access to resources, research performance, and rewards . . . especially between younger men and women" (Zuckerman 1991, 28). This appears to hold true for psychology's younger women. Of the 30 APA awards going to women for distinguished contributions since 1976, 14 have been granted for an Early Career Contribution to Psychology (Scarborough, 1992).

In addition to persisting differences in performance and growing convergence in access, Zuckerman also identified a third pattern operating at present: "*growing divergence* between men and women of the same professional age in published productivity and in some, but not all, aspects of career attainment; that is, growing intra-cohort differences [in published productivity and career attainment] as members move through their careers" (Zuckerman 1991, 28). Let us hope that the third pattern may be negated for our younger colleagues as they develop their careers. And perhaps we ourselves can reverse the pattern as it has been followed until just recently in historical studies, so that the growing divergence, over time, between accomplished men and women in the attention given them in history of psychology texts might be arrested.

REFERENCES

ABIR-AM, P. & D. OUTRAM. 1987. Uneasy Careers and Intimate Lives. Rutgers University Press. New Brunswick, NJ.

BORING, E. G. 1961. Psychologist at Large: An Autobiography and Selected Essays. Basic Books. New York.

CAPSHEW, J. H. & E. R. HILGARD. 1992. The power of service: World War II and professional reform in the American Psychological Association. In The American Psychological Association: A Historical Perspective. R. B. Evans, V. S. Sexton & T. C. Cadwallader, Eds.: 149–175. American Psychological Association. Washington, DC.

COLE, J. R. 1979. Fair Science: Women in the Scientific Community. Free Press. New York.

EBERTS, C. G. & P. H. GRAY. 1982. Evaluating the historical treatment of female psychologists of distinction using citation analysis and textbook coverage. Bull. Psychonom. Soc. 20: 7–10.

FERBER, M. 1986. Citations: Are they an objective measure of work of women and men? Signs. 11: 381–389.

FERNBERGER, S. W. 1928. Statistical analyses of the members and associates of the American Psychological Association, Inc. in 1928. Psychol. Rev. 35: 447–465.

FURUMOTO, L. 1988. Shared knowledge: The experimentalists, 1904–1929. In The Rise of Experimentation in American Psychology. J. G. Morawski, Ed.: 94–113. Yale University Press. New Haven, CT.

GLAZER, P. M. & M. SLATER. 1987. Unequal colleagues: The entrance of women into the professions, 1890–1940. Rutgers University Press. New Brunswick, NJ.

HAGSTROM, W. O. 1965. The Scientific Community. Basic Books. New York.

HELMREICH, R. L. & J. T. SPENCE. 1982. Gender differences in productivity and impact. Am. Psychologist 37: 1142.

HELMREICH, R. L., J. T. SPENCE, W. E. BEANE, G. W. LUCKER & K. A. MATTHEWS. 1980. Making it in academic psychology: Demographic and personality correlates of attainment. J. Pers. Soc. Psychol. 39: 896–908.

KASS-SIMON, G., P. FARNES & D. NASH., Eds. 1990. Women in Science: Righting the Record. Indiana University Press. Bloomington, IN.

MUEHLENHARD, C. L. 1992. Women and men: New—and not so new—perspectives on gender differences. Contemp. Psychol. 37: 123–124.

O'CONNELL, A. N. & N. F. RUSSO, Eds. 1983. Models of Achievement: Reflections of Eminent Women in Psychology. Columbia University Press. New York.

O'CONNELL, A. N. & N. F. RUSSO, Eds. 1988. Models of Achievement: Reflections of Eminent Women in Psychology. Vol. 2. Lawrence Erlbaum. Hillsdale, NJ.

O'CONNELL, A. N. & N. F. RUSSO, Eds. 1990. Women in Psychology: A Bio-bibliographic Sourcebook. Greenwood Press. New York.

O'CONNELL, A. N. & N. F. RUSSO, Eds. 1991. Women's heritage in psychology: Origins, development, and future directions, Vol. 15. Psychology of Women Quarterly.

ROSENBERG, R. 1982. Beyond Separate Spheres: Intellectual Roots of Modern Feminism. Yale University Press. New Haven, CT.

ROSSITER, M. W. 1982. Women scientists in America: Struggles and Strategies to 1940. The Johns Hopkins University Press. Baltimore, MD.

RUSSETT, C. E. 1989. Sexual Science, the Construction of Womanhood. Harvard University Press. Cambridge, MA.

SCARBOROUGH, E. 1992. Women in the American Psychological Association. *In* The American Psychological Association: A Historical Perspective. R. B. Evans, V. S. Sexton & T. C. Cadwallader, Eds.: 303–325. American Psychological Association. Washington, DC.

SCARBOROUGH, E. & L. FURUMOTO. 1987. Untold lives: The First Generation of American Women Psychologists. Columbia University Press. New York.

SCHIEBINGER, L. 1989. The Mind Has No Sex? Women in the Origins of Modern Science. Harvard University Press. Cambridge, MA.

ZUCKERMAN, H. 1991. The careers of men and women scientists: A review of current research. *In* The Outer Circle: Women in the Scientific Community. H. Zuckerman, J. R. Cole & J. T. Bruer, Eds.: 27–56. Norton. New York.

ZUCKERMAN, H. & J. R. COLE. 1975. Women in American science. Minerva **13:** 82–102.

ZUCKERMAN, H., J. R. COLE & J. T. BRUER., Eds. 1991. The Outer Circle: Women in the Scientific Community. Norton. New York.

The European Influence on American Psychology: 1892 and 1942

HELMUT E. ADLER

Department of Psychology
Yeshiva University
New York, New York 10033

A century is a long time; a century is a short time. In 1892 Benjamin Harrison was president. It was a presidential election year. The Democratic candidate, Grover Cleveland, defeated the Republic incumbent to gain his second term. There were no automobiles, airplanes, telephones, radio, or television. For a psychologist, it was an advantage to have a Ph.D. from a German university. Women, Blacks, Jews, and the handicapped were discriminated against.

1992 was again a presidential election year. An incumbent Republican had to defend his administration. We have automobiles, airplanes, telephones, radio, and television, but women, Blacks, Jews, and the handicapped still have a hard time. And for psychologists, it is now a disadvantage to have a Ph.D. from a German university.

This paper will consider some of the changes that have influenced psychology during this 100-year period as an organized profession. As the focus of this discussion, we shall look at some of the factors responsible both for the changes that have taken place, as well as for the invariables that have persisted over this period. For purposes of this comparison, we shall examine the years 1892 and, a half-century later, the year 1942. Hindsight is clearer at a distance.

The world of 1892 was a world of peace, stability, and certainty. The world of 1942 was a world of war, instability, and uncertainty. In 1892 the second International Congress of Psychology convened in London, England. In 1942 Heinrich Himmler and cohorts held a conference in Wannsee, a Berlin suburb, to decide on the so-called "final solution." In 1892 E. B. Titchener received his Ph.D. in Leipzig; in 1942 Seymour Sarason completed his doctorate at Clark University. In 1892, William James published *Psychology: The Briefer Course*; and, while he might have published it in 1942, Clark Lee Hull actually published his *Principles of Behavior* in 1943. These historical landmarks characterize their periods. 1892 was a beginning, a time when psychological laboratories were still being founded—at Yale by Ladd and Scripture and at Brown by Delabarre for example. It was the year the Münsterberg took over the Harvard laboratory. The year before had seen the

113

beginnings of laboratory psychology laid down at Columbia by Cattell, at Wellesley by Mary Calkins, at Cornell by Frank Angell, and at Catholic University in Washington, D.C., by E. A. Pace. And in the next year, 1893, departments were being started at Princeton by Baldwin, at Stanford by F. Angell, at Minnesota by James Rowland Angell, and at Chicago by John Dewey and F. Angell (Hilgard 1987).

The common thread that connected these events was the importation of ideas from Germany and, in most cases, but not all, from Wundt's Leipzig laboratory, either directly, as was the case (for example) with Scripture, F. Angell, Münsterberg, and Cattell, or indirectly by Calkins, via Hall and Delabarre through Münsterberg. A German Ph.D. was the key to a good position in an American university of the first rank.

When G. Stanley Hall called together a group of psychologists in his study on 8 July 1892 to launch a psychological association, a majority followed the German model, although only Cattell had a Leipzig degree. Hall and Baldwin had visited Leipzig, but taken their degrees at home. James, Jastrow, and Ladd were of course only indirectly affected. And James, although absent at this occasion, had already expressed his opinion about a science so dreary that only a German could stomach it (Adler 1992). When the first meeting of the new American Psychological Association took place in Philadelphia, on 27 December 1992, at the University of Pennsylvania, the first slate of officers included Hall as president, Jastrow as secretary-treasurer, and a council of Baldwin, Cattell, James, Ladd, and G. S. Fullerton, as well as J.G. Schurman, a philosopher at Cornell. Respectively, these individuals represented Clark, Wisconsin, Toronto, Columbia, Harvard, Yale, Pennsylvania, and Cornell, a veritable roll call of mostly Eastern establishment universities (Hilgard 1987). Many of the attendees were later also elected to the APA's presidency: Hall (a second time), James (twice), Ladd (1893), Cattell (1895), Fullerton (1896), and Baldwin (1897). Altogether, the fledgling APA had 31 members in 1892 (Dennis and Boring 1952).

One may wonder what happened to Titchener, Wundt's most vocal supporter. He only had arrived at Cornell in 1892 and was immediately elected a member of the APA (membership was by invitation). He resigned, however, in 1897, over a dispute about Scripture's plagiarizing of Titchener's work and Creighton's translation of Wundt's *Vorlesungen über die Menschen- und Thierseele* [*Lectures on the Human and the Animal Mind*] published by Wundt in 1892, with the translation published in 1894. In 1904, Titchener wanted an exclusive club, a smoke-filled room, no women members. The Clark group—Sanford, Boring, and Baird—and Harvard's Holt and Langfeld joined. The Society of Experimental Psychologists, as the group was called, also included Münsterberg, who was not eager to belong, Judd at Yale, and Witmer at Pennsylvania, until he too dropped out. Boring (1967), who wrote up this history, also relates that Titchener feuded with

Hollingworth, whose review of Titchener's textbook insulted him, and with Woodworth, who offended him when he posted his invitation, normally to be treasured, on the bulletin board with the note: "Who wants to go?" Boring also relates an illuminating anecdote about Christine Ladd-Franklin, who was eager to present her color-vision theory. At the 1914 meeting she and Al Poffenberger were locked in a room, so she could not attend the meeting. (She apparently did attend, however, on another occasion.) (Boring 1967)

In the '90s psychology was much in demand as an academic discipline. University administrators vied with each other to attract knowledgeable instructors of the "New Psychology." Although they sometimes were reluctant to support requests for laboratory equipment, laboratories nonetheless proliferated, under the rubric that "it was the right thing to do." By the year 1900 there were already more psychology laboratories in the United States than chairs of psychology in Germany (Ash 1982). And by 1903 the nearly 50 departments by then in existence had produced some 100 doctorates in psychology (Benjamin 1986). At first, a German Ph.D. or at least some semesters of study abroad were the keys to success. But gradually the psychology that was taught and researched in this country deviated from the European model as it was modified by the American environment. As Rieber (1980) put it: "The relationship between Wundt's system and American psychology may best be described as an affair that runs its course from flirtation to abandonment."

As the years progressed, other factors came into play. One was a growing negative attitude against "foreigners." Of course America (apart from the Indians) is a country of foreigners who arrived in successive influxes of migration (Commager 1961). Each wave of immigrants objected to the next push, usually triggered by some events in Europe. In 1921 the first quota laws were established, with 357,000 immigrants permitted yearly. In 1924, this number was reduced to 150,000. In addition, in the years leading up to World War I and for some years afterward, anti-German feelings were widespread. Today we consider World War I one of the most unnecessary of wars, but in 1916 the American public was led by propaganda and commercial interests into what amounted to mass hysteria. It was the time when sauerkraut became "victory cabbage" and Dachshunds were persecuted.

During the period between the two wars, American psychology was thriving, but much of its development was ostensibly not influenced by Europe. This is not the place to show the roots of the positivism, operationism, behaviorism, and mechanism that came to dominate American psychology. They surely can be found in European forerunners. But we do want to look at 1942 and the state of psychology at that time.

Innovative ideas published in this year were to be found in Freeman and

Watts' *Prefrontal Lobotomy,* Sheldon and Stevens' *Varieties of Temperament,* and Carl Rogers' exposition of client-centered psychotherapy. The APA met in New York City that year. C. P. Stone was president, W. C. Olson was secretary, and W. L. Valentine was treasurer. The council consisted of E. A. Culler, H. B. English, J. P. Guilford, E. R. Guthrie, E. Heidbreder, and E. R. Hilgard. Guthrie and Hilgard were future APA presidents in 1945 and 1949, respectively. These were all experimentalists. Only after World War II did clinicians appear in larger numbers. Notable by their absence were Gestalt psychologists and psychoanalysts.

Actually, as Sokal (1988) notes, Wolfgang Köhler, one of Gestalt psychology's founders, had contact with Yerkes as early as 1914, reflecting their common interest in anthropoid apes. Köhler lectured at Clark University in 1925, as arranged by Murchison. And in 1934 Köhler gave the William James lecture at Harvard. Eventually Köhler was forced to leave Berlin, where he had been professor of psychology, under pressure from Nazi sympathizers among students and faculty, as the result of his opposition to the persecution and dismissal of his colleagues. When he emigrated to America, he did not get an appointment at Harvard, for which he had been considered, but settled at Swarthmore College, an undergraduate institution and thus without Ph.D. students. Köhler was jointed by Hans Wallach, his former student in Berlin and his collaborator at Swarthmore in research on visual perception. Among the predoctoral and postdoctoral researchers he attracted, Mary Henle became an advocate of the cause of Gestalt psychology, as well as a curator of Köhler's legacy (Henle 1971).

Kurt Koffka, who had introduced Gestalt theory to American psychologists in 1922 with his paper "Perception: An introduction to *Gestalt-Theorie,*" settled at Smith College in Northhampton, Massachusetts, where he gave only one Ph.D., to Molly Harrower (Henle 1980). Koffka was also able to bring from Europe such important followers as Fritz Heider, Alexander Mintz, Tamara Dembo, and Eugenia Hanfmann.

Max Wertheimer, the first of Gestalt psychology's founders, was able to find a position at the New School for Social Research in New York City, an institution specially designed to employ refugees from Europe, but one that did not, at first, have graduate students and give graduate degrees, although eventually he did attract some distinguished students. His associates Karl Duncker, Solomon Asch, George Katona, and Rudolf Arnheim influenced American psychology. His student Abraham S. Luchins, not an emigré, also had an unmistakable impact on psychological theory (Mandler and Mandler 1969).

Kurt Lewin came to America in 1932, first being associated with Stanford University, then with Cornell University, next with the University of Iowa, and finally with MIT, but could establish himself at first only with great difficulties. Kurt Goldstein, who had briefly been put into a concentration camp in 1933, left immediately on his release for Amsterdam. Here he wrote his chief work, *The Organism,* before coming to American in 1935. He was the William James lecturer at Harvard in 1938–1939. He held clinical professorships at Columbia's Psychiatric Institute, at Tufts Medical School, at City College of New York, and at Brandeis University, but never established a following of his own. He was in private practice, and after his wife died in 1960, a cousin, Betty Falk, moved in to take care of him (Simmel 1966).

The history of psychoanalysis in America is too well known to repeat here. Freud and Jung were well enough known to be invited by G. S. Hall to the 20th anniversary festivities at Clark in 1909. It may not be so well known that Wundt had been Hall's first choice and that Freud had originally turned down the invitation because he had not been offered as much money as Wundt (Evans and Koelsch 1985). When the Nazi persecutions forced numerous psychoanalysts to emigrate, many came to the United States. Erich Fromm, Karen Horney, Alfred Adler, and Wilhelm Reich come to mind. A more complete list is given in Welleck (1968) (see also the Appendix to this article). They collected disciples, but were not part of the established scientific community. Conflict between academicians and psychoanalysts was not new. In pre-Anschluss Vienna, Karl Bühler, professor of psychology at Vienna University, never met Sigmund Freud in person, although they had lived in the same city for seventeen years (Jahoda 1960). There was also the objection by the medical profession to the practice of psychoanalytic therapy by nonmedical therapists. Behind this nonacceptance there lay an unspoken discrimination against outsiders, foreigners and Jews, in many cases.

In addition to Gestalt psychologists and psychoanalysts, many other psychologists who had a European reputation often had great difficulties in re-establishing their careers in America. When he arrived in the U.S., Karl Bühler suffered from neglect. Since none of his major works had been translated into English, he was relatively unknown. His students, such as Egon Brunswik, Edward C. Tolman, René Spitz, and Else Frenkel-Brunswik did, however, influence American thought. On the other hand, his wife, Charlotte Bühler, who outlived him by many years, had a major impact on developmental psychology (Mandler and Mandler 1969).

William Stern, a founder of the University of Hamburg and the originator of the concept of the IQ, came to Duke University in 1934. On account of his early death, his influence was exerted primarily via his students Heinz Werner and Martin Scheerer. Heinz Werner's career typifies the problems even a well-known European emigré had in finding permanent employment. After his dismissal from the Hamburg faculty, he came to the University of Michigan on the invitation of Walter Pillsbury, though not as a regular faculty member. In 1936 he became senior research scientist at the Wayne

County Training School, where he stayed until 1943, except for a visiting professorship at Harvard during 1936–1937. In 1943 he was appointed instructor at Brooklyn College. Eventually, in 1947, he became a professor at Clark University, where he was finally able to establish himself in a position of influence. His sensory-tonic theory became an important point of view in the theory of perception (Mandler and Mandler 1969).

Martin Scheerer first worked at Montefiore Hospital in New York, developing with Kurt Goldstein the Goldstein–Scheerer test of abstract thinking. After some short stays at Wells College, Brooklyn College, and the City College of New York, he eventually wound up at the University of Kansas (Mandler and Mandler 1969).

Wellek (1968) lists well-known social psychologists displaced by the Nazis and contributing important research in the United States. The list includes Paul Lazarsfeld, who found his position in Austria intolerable as early as 1933. As he put it: "Under the adverse economic circumstances in Austria and the strong current of incipient anti-Semitism, a regular academic career would have been almost impossible" (Lazarsfeld 1969). Originally supported by the Rockefeller Foundation, he eventually founded his own Bureau of Applied Social Research at Columbia University, changing his field from psychology to sociology in the process.

Despite great difficulties, these eminent emigrés eventually established new careers in their American refuge. It should be mentioned that in 1938 the American Psychological Association had established a Committee on Displaced Foreign Psychologists. The committee was chaired by Barbara S. Burks from its beginnings to her death in 1943. The APA had contributed $50 to a total funding of some $580 in the overall budget of the committee. Nevertheless it circulated a list of 111 "displaced foreign scholars," not all of whom had yet been able to emigrate. Those that did arrive were interviewed and an attempt was made to place them. The total number that reached the United States was 159 (Mandler and Mandler 1969, 383). The Rockefeller Foundation had also been active, providing for placement of immigrant psychologists. In particular, it sponsored the New School for Social Research, which functioned as a "university-in-exile" for many European scholars, including some eminent psychologists.

The openings for academicians were very scarce in the thirties and forties. Unemployed American psychologists competed with European immigrants for the same positions. As the Burks committee noted in its report for 1941: "Only a small proportion either in this or other countries are in jobs commensurate with their training and experience" (Mandler and Mandler 1969, 383). The notable fact is, however, that most of the eminent immigrants did eventually find employment, even if not in positions equivalent to those held in Europe. A list of 300 notable emigrés in Fleming and Baylin's *The Intellectual Migration* (1969) includes a total of 30 psychologists and psychoanalysts (*see* the Appendix). The list is by no means complete, but indicative of the fate of a considerable number of psychologists and psychoanalysts whose prominence was unquestioned. In addition to this group we must recognize the immigrant psychologists who had not yet reached the level of visibility that merited inclusion in the list. These had been assistants or Ph.D. candidates in well-known European universities. They had to find whatever employment they could after arrival in the United States. Only after considerable struggle was it possible for some of them to find suitable employment and to complete their education.

This brings me back to the beginning of this paper. In 50 years there has been change. Americans had absorbed the European ideas and developed them in ways that were only foreshadowed by the original founders. And, below the surface, there still was prejudice, conservatism, fear of novel ideas, and a growing mistrust of foreigners. Since this period coincided with the forced emigration of many well-qualified European-trained psychologists (and to some extent psychoanalysts), it made it particularly difficult for these individuals to establish themselves in American academia. Whereas in 1892 a German Ph.D. was the key to an academic career, in 1942, the door tended to be closed and the European Ph.D.s could only knock on the door, often in vain.

The next 50 years would bring new attitudes. The world shrunk through better communication and transportation. Psychology became more international. American psychological theories became dominant in Europe and in Germany in particular. At the same time, the European influence made itself felt in American psychology. Many of the individuals mentioned in this essay eventually became absorbed into mainstream psychology and contributed significant new ideas and approaches. A one-world point of view prevailed. Attitudes had come full circle. Will they go once more beyond the current open state? Will the cycle continue? Where will it end?

REFERENCES

ADLER, H. E. 1992. William James and Gustav Fechner: From rejection to elective affinity. *In* Reinterpreting the Legacy of William James. M. E. Donnelly, Ed. American Psychological Association. Washington, DC.

ASH, M. G. 1982. Reflections on psychology in history. *In* The Problematic Science: Psychology in Nineteenth Century Thought. W. R. Woodward & M. G. Ash, Eds. Praeger. New York.

BENJAMIN, L. T., JR. 1986. Why don't they understand us? A history of psychology's public image. Am. Psychol. **41:** 941–946.

BORING, E. G. 1967. Titchener's experimentalists. J. Hist. Behav. Sci. **2:** 315–325.

COMMAGER, H. S. 1961. Immigration and American History. University of Minnesota Press. Minneapolis, MN.

DENNIS, W. & E. G. BORING. 1952. The founding of the APA. Am. Psychol. 7: 95–97.
EVANS, R. B. & W. A. KOELSCH. 1985. Psychoanalysis arrives in America: The 1909 psychology conference at Clark University. Am. Psychol. 40: 942–948.
FLEMING, D. & B. BAILYN, Eds. 1969. The Intellectual Migration: Europe and America, 1930–1960. Harvard University Press. Cambridge, MA.
FREEMAN, W. & J. W. WATTS. 1942. Psychosurgery. Intelligence, Emotion and Social Behavior following Prefrontal Lobotomy for Mental Disorders. Charles C Thomas. Springfield, IL.
GOLDSTEIN, K. 1939. The Organism. American Book Co. New York.
HENLE, M. 1971. The Selected Papers of Wolfgang Köhler. Liveright. New York.
HENLE, M. 1980. The influence of Gestalt psychology in America. In Psychology: Theoretical-historical Perspectives. R. Rieber & K. Salzinger, Eds. Academic Press. New York.
HILGARD, E. R. 1987. Psychology in America: A Historical Survey. Harcourt, Brace, Jovanovich. New York.
HULL, C. L. 1943. Principles of Behavior. Appleton-Century. New York.
JAHODA, M. 1960. The migration of psychoanalysis: Its impact on American psychology. In The Intellectual Migration: Europe and America, 1930–1960. D. Fleming & B. Bailyn, Eds. Harvard University Press. Cambridge, MA.
JAMES, W. 1892. Psychology: The Briefer Course. Holt. New York.
LAZARSFELD, P. F. 1969. An episode in the history of social research: A memoir. In The Intellectual Migration: Europe and America, 1930–1960. D. Fleming & B. Bailyn, Eds. Harvard University Press. Cambridge, MA.
MANDLER, J. M. & G. MANDLER. 1969. The diaspora of experimental psychology: The Gestaltists and others. In The Intellectual Migration: Europe and America, 1930–1960. D. Fleming & B. Bailyn, Eds. Harvard University Press. Cambridge, MA.
RIEBER, R. W. 1980. Wundt and the Americans: From flirtation to abandonment. In Wilhelm Wundt and the Making of Scientific Psychology. R. W. Rieber, Ed. Plenum Press. New York.
ROGERS, C. R. 1942. Counseling and Psychotherapy. Houghton Mifflin. Boston, MA.
SHELDON, W. H. & S. S. STEVENS. 1942. The Varieties of Temperament: A Psychology of Constitutional Differences. Harper. New York.
SIMMEL, M. 1966. Obituary: Kurt Goldstein 1878–1965. J. Hist. Behav. Sci. 2: 185–191.
SOKAL, M. M. 1988. The Gestalt psychologists in behaviorist America. In A History of Psychology L. T. Benjamin, Jr., Ed. McGraw-Hill, New York.
WELLEK, A. 1968. The impact of the German immigration on the development of American psychology. J. Hist. Behav. Sci. 4: 207–229.

APPENDIX

The following eminent emigré psychologists and psychoanalysts are listed among 300 notable emigrés in Fleming and Bailyn (1969).

ADORNO, THEODOR. Social scientist. Research on *The Authoritarian Personality* 1941–1949.

ALEXANDER, FRANZ. Psychoanalyst. Pioneer in psychosomatic illness.

ARHNEIM, RUDOLF. Psychologist. New School for Social Research (New York) 1943–1968; Sarah Lawrence College 1943–1968; Harvard University from 1968; Guggenheim Fellow 1942–1943.

BETTELHEIM, BRUNO. Psychoanalyst. Research associate, University of Chicago 1939–1941; Associate professor, Rockford College 1942–1944; eventually professor, University of Chicago.

BIBRING, GRETE LEHNER. Psychoanalyst. Student of Freud. Boston Psychoanalytical Society and Institute from 1941; Faculty, Harvard Medical School 1946–1965.

BRUNSWIK, EGON. Psychologist. Rockefeller Foundation Fellow 1935–1936; faculty, University of California, Berkeley 1937–1955.

BÜHLER, CHARLOTTE. Psychologist. Taught at College of St. Catherine (St. Paul, Minnesota) 1940–1941; visiting professor, Clark University 1941–1942; clinical psychologist, Minneapolis General Hospital 1942–1945; private practice from 1945.

BÜHLER, KARL. Psychologist. College of St. Thomas (St. Paul, Minnesota) 1940–1945; private practice 1945–1956.

DEUTSCH, HELENE. Psychoanalyst. Member, Boston Psychoanalytical Institute from 1937.

DICHTER, ERNEST. Psychologist. Research psychologist with J. Stirling Getchell, advertising agency; president, Institute for Motivational Research.

ERIKSON, ERIK HOMBURGER. Psychoanalyst. Research, Harvard Medical School 1934–1935; Yale School of Medicine 1936–1939; University of California, Berkeley and San Francisco 1939–1951. Staff, Austin Riggs Center (Stockbridge, MA) 1951–1960; professor, Human Development, Harvard University from 1960.

FENICHEL, OTTO. Psychoanalyst. Private practice, Los Angeles from 1938.

FRENKEL-BRUNSWIK, ELSE. Psychologist. Research associate, Institute for Child Welfare, Berkeley, 1939–1958.

FROMM, ERICH. Psychoanalyst. Bennington College 1941–1950; National Autonomous University of Mexico from 1951.

FROMM-REICHMANN, FRIEDA. Psychoanalyst. Fellow, William Alanson White Institute of Psychiatry and Psychoanalysis 1943–1957.

GOLDSTEIN, KURT. Neuropsychiatrist. Montefiore Hospital 1936–1940; Tufts Medical School 1940–1945; City College of New York 1950–1955; New School for Social Research 1955–1965.

HARTMANN, HEINZ. Psychoanalyst. Training analysis with Freud. New York Psychoanalytic Institute 1948–1951 and private practice.

HEIDER, FRITZ. Psychologist. Faculty, Smith College 1930–1947; professor, University of Kansas from 1947.

HERZOG, HERTA. Psychologist. Office of Radio Research, Princeton 1938–1941; Bureau of Applied Social Research, Columbia University 1935–1943; McCann-Erickson advertising agency 1943–1961; partner, Jack Tinker and Partners advertising agency from 1962.

HORNEY, KAREN. Psychoanalyst. Associate director, Chicago Institute of Psychoanalysis; lecturer, New School for Social Research from 1935; Dean, American Institute for Psychoanalysis (New York) from 1941.

JAHODA, MARIE. Psychologist. Research associate, American Jewish Committee 1945–1948; Bureau of Applied Social Research, Columbia University, 1948–1959; New York University 1949–1958, becoming professor of psychology and director of the Research Center for Human Relations.

KRIS, ERNST. Psychoanalyst. New School for Social Research 1940–1945; visiting professor, City College of New York; Child Study Center, Yale Medical School 1949–1957.

LAZARSFELD, PAUL F. Psychologist/sociologist. Rockefeller Foundation Fellow 1933; director, Research Center University of Newark 1935–1937; director, Office of Radio Research, Princeton University; director and chairman, Bureau of Applied Social Research, Columbia University 1939; professor of psychology, later of sociology, Columbia University.

LEWIN, KURT. Psychologist. Visiting professor of psychology, Stanford University 1932–1933; acting professor, Cornell University 1933–1935; professor of child psychology, University of Iowa 1935–1944; professor and director, Research Center for Group Dynamics, Massachusetts Institute of Technology 1944–1947.

REDL, FRITZ. Psychoanalyst. Research associate, General Education Board, Rockefeller Foundation; lecturer in mental hygiene, University of Michigan 1938–1941; professor of social work, Wayne State University 1941–1953; chief, Child Research Bureau, NIH (Bethesda, MD) 1953–1959; professor of behavioral sciences, Wayne State University from 1953.

REICH, WILHELM. Psychoanalyst. Lecturer, New School for Social Research 1940–1942; established "Orgone" energy laboratory; ignored injunction by Food and Drug Administration, died in jail in Washington, DC, 1957.

REIK, THEODOR. Psychoanalyst. Director, Society for Psychoanalytic Psychology, New York, from 1941; professor, Adelphi University (Garden City, NY).

STERN, WILLIAM. Psychologist. Lecturer, then professor, Duke University 1934–1938.

WERNER, HEINZ. Psychologist. Lecturer, University of Michigan 1933–1936; research associate, Harvard University 1936–1937; Wayne County Training School (Michigan) 1937–1944; instructor, Brooklyn College 1945–1947; professor, Clark University from 1947.

WERTHEIMER, MAX. Psychologist. Professor, New School for Social Research 1934–1943.

Historical Perspectives
on Psychotherapy

DONALD K. FREEDHEIM
Department of Psychology
Case Western Reserve University
Cleveland, Ohio 44106

The field of psychotherapy has grown rapidly and with great diversity over this century. Many of its developments can hardly be viewed in a historical context, as some specialties have barely spanned a generation in time. The originators of many training methods and techniques are still studying and researching them. On the other hand, the roots of what we generally term psychotherapy—that is, the use of verbal interaction and interpersonal relationship to effect positive change—go deep into human history. One can certainly imagine the use of interpersonal persuasion to influence thoughts, feelings, and behavior as long as humans have been able to communicate with one another. But it is of interest that it is only in the latter part of the last century that we have begun to bring such interactions into a "therapeutic" context, in which we pay another individual, outside family and friends, to alleviate mental and emotional problems. Prior to that time, prophets, philosophers, priests, and perhaps even politicians were seen as the "persuaders" of our behavior.

Perhaps as humans have come to live closer together, with the dual expectations of freedom to chose one's destiny and of independence or self-sufficiency, that our need to relate on a one-to-one basis has dictated the shift from group persuasion to interpersonal influence. Psychotherapy has certainly provided the means to have close, interpersonal contact with someone, while achieving great feats of individualism and independence. Cushman (1992) has pointed out that much of the role of psychotherapy in the current century has been to "heal the personal interiority within each self-contained individual . . ." (p. 57). Further, he comments, "The private interior needs to be protected, understood, cared for, healed, and made to thrive" (p. 57). And it is psychotherapy's job to do just that.

For the greater portion of our history, the culture of Western society has been the major influence on our field. Only recently have we come to recognize and integrate the contributions that Eastern philosophies can have on our field. In fact, only portions of our so-called Western civilization have been welcome contributors to the field. As the *History of Psychotherapy: A Century of Change* (Freedheim 1992) so painfully points out, there have been periods when American psychology has systematically excluded contributions of women and of ethnic minorities. This was—and perhaps still is in the latter case—a function of the mores of the times. How often have we seen professional groups rise to force institutional change against the prevailing cultural or even political tide?

It is clear that the field of psychotherapy, from research laboratories to clinical offices, has been primarily responsive to the social and economic forces in our society. This is not to imply that the findings of research, the needs of patients, and the individual interests of professionals are negligible factors in the evolution of the field. Many of the trends in therapeutic developments have been logical results of objective observations. But these have always been manifested and interpreted in the context of the times.

In this limited space, I would like to highlight some of the turning points in the development of psychotherapy which have influenced the field. These will be divided into theory, research, practice, and training.

THEORY

The starting point for most historians of psychotherapy is the work of Sigmund Freud. The extension of the drive theory to include the ego was begun by Freud early in his development, together with the concept of defense (Eagle and Wolitzky 1992). Just after the turn of the century, the id became the focus of Freud's theoretical writings, and the period following World War I saw the development of "ego psychology." For approximately three decades (1940–1970), ego psychology predominated in analytic writing. In the last two decades, the two main streams of psychoanalytic theory have come from object relations theory and formulations relating to the self, as represented by Kohut (Eagle and Wolitzky 1992).

Less familiar may be the evolution in behavioral theory and practice. Developments in this framework may be characterized as fanning out from its basic S-R (stimulus-response) principles, as opposed to the more linear developments in the dynamic sphere (Fishman and Franks, 1992).

Watsonian behaviorism was a radical departure from the theoretical models popular in psychology at that time, as it rejected mentalistic models, social context, and intention as motivators for behavior. Instead, humans— although complex organisms—were driven by stimulus-response relationships, which could best be demonstrated in the laboratory with animals (Fishman and Franks 1992). Until the 1950s, the behavioral field was dominated by theorists who founded the laws of learning, basic to the scientific (i.e., experimental) underpinnings of our discipline.

At mid-century, many psychologists turned to the task of solving human problems, now using principles which had been developed in the laboratory.

Behavior modification proved to be a successful method for training retarded children and for dealing with severe behavior problems (Azrin 1977).

One of the important breakthroughs in behavioral work was the development of the technique of systematic desensitization (Wolpe 1958), which launched behavioral techniques beyond simple reward systems to a "talking" therapy within the behavioral framework. This technique was soon followed by social modeling (Bandura 1982), cognitive behavior therapy, and similar therapeutic models designed to change negative thinking patterns.

At the almost opposite end of the spectrum, humanistic theories began to play an important role in the understanding of behavior and interpersonal relationships. As a "third force" in psychology, humanism derived its meaning from uniquely human modes of functioning, which were particularly relevant to the experience of psychotherapy (Rice and Greenberg 1992).

Based upon philosophical treatises, the origins of the humanistic approach were largely developed and nurtured by Carl Rogers, who first enunciated its principles in the early 1940s (Rogers 1942). Following Rogers (although independent of his work), existential approaches emerged in Europe, mainly fostered by analysts who believed the person was being lost in the analytic process (Rice and Greenberg 1992). Soon the principles enunciated by the early gestalt phenomenologists were loosely incorporated into a gestalt psychotherapy, which focused on the "whole" of the person and aimed at maximizing the potential of the individual.

Emerging from the various theoretical positions is the current emphasis on integrative approaches to formulate principles of therapy. Early on, the integrative approach to psychotherapy sought ways to combine psychoanalytic and behavioral approaches. More recently, theoretical integration has meant the combining of any of several means to explain behavior or the search for common factors among various approaches to therapy (Arkowitz 1992).

Clearly, the theoretical formulations alluded to above are sketchy and incomplete. Readers who would like to explore these and other theoretical foundations of psychotherapy will find a thorough review in Freedheim 1992.

RESEARCH

The importance of research in psychotherapy is inherent in the work of virtually all psychologists. Early in graduate training, we are taught the values of systematically testing hypotheses and theories about all aspects of behavior, including personality development and the possible changes in personality and behavior brought about by psychotherapy. The great question underlying all our endeavors in psychotherapy is, "Does it work?" Is it effective as an agent of change? This question pervades the thinking of all of the researchers who have explored the various aspects of psychotherapy.

The problem for researchers in this field is the paucity of techniques for adequate study. Unlike other scientific disciplines, some of which have developed very sophisticated techniques (e.g., electron microscopy), psychology must study communication and behavioral change, which do not lend themselves to such beautiful methods. Measuring the results of psychotherapy is a little like measuring a moving snake with a ruler.

Perhaps the first report on the outcome of therapy was published in 1930 (Fenichel 1930) by the Berlin Psychoanalytic Institute, a study in which over 700 analyses were considered. Of these, 241 patients had dropped out and 117 were still in progress. Of the 363 completed therapies, 111 were deemed cured; 89, very improved; 116 improved; and 47 not cured. The writer claimed a broad range of effectiveness: from 60–90%, which was perhaps modest under the circumstances. Clearly, this research was vitiated due to selection effects, but it at least attempted to ascertain the effectiveness of therapeutic procedures in some systematic manner.

Early in the development of research centers in this country to study the effects of psychotherapy, an English psychologist reported that patients engaged in therapy fared no better or no worse than those on waiting lists for treatment (Eysenck 1952). This finding dealt quite a blow to the early researchers in the field and one might say that we have been trying to prove Eysenck wrong ever since. Actually, research in psychotherapy has targeted many aspects of the subject, including interactions between therapist and client, methodological approaches, and effects of psychotropic drugs.

In terms of effectiveness, we have gotten away from the traditional "ballpark figure" of two-thirds effectiveness (Eysenck 1952) to rates calculated in more statistically sophisticated terms. A fairly recent meta-analysis of outcome studies (Smith et al. 1980) has derived overall effectiveness in the 80% range for studies which have acceptable validity in the field.

The first attempts to study, in any systematic way, the process of psychotherapy were made just prior to the Second World War. In the mid-1940s, the Menninger Clinic developed a comprehensive research program to evaluate the effectiveness of psychotherapy. Using novel statistical techniques, the work has continued to the present day. The latest publication from the study is a comprehensive 40-year follow-up (Wallerstein 1986). Many of the researchers in the early years of the Menninger project went on to found their own centers or have collaborated on large projects (Strupp and Howard 1992).

Among the early pioneers in psychotherapy research, Jerome Frank has been a teacher and model for many of the leading researchers of today. He has briefly summarized his work (Frank 1992) and concluded that the most important finding has been the shift in emphasis from the techniques in therapy to the personal features of the therapist, the patient, and the relationship between them. This theme is repeated throughout most of the findings of research centers studying the effects of therapy, although recently focus has been turned to comparing long and short terms of therapy on specific problem groups.

PRACTICE

Where did the "practice" of psychotherapy begin? This is an unanswerable question in the absence of clear definitions of "practice" and of "psychotherapy." Most therapists identify Freud's work in Vienna as the primary site for the practice of psychotherapy, although it could be well argued that our practice goes much further back in history.

In the United States, we generally attribute the beginnings of our practice to the clinic of Lightner Witmer in 1896 (Cattell 1954). The initial client in that setting was a child with a learning problem (possibly retardation) and the outcome was not a dramatic one (Brotemarkle 1947).

Since this early case, the question of outcome in psychotherapy has been at the forefront of practice issues. Even today, we have not arrived at adequate criteria for determining success of psychotherapy. The fact that there are so many variations of practice, even within fairly well-defined approaches, only complicates the situation.

Through the last 100 years of practice work, the legality of practitioners (psychologists, social workers, etc.) has been a major issue of contention. For much of the century, psychiatry dominated the field, but shifts toward medication by psychiatry, licensing laws, and public education and awareness have brought greater recognition of psychology and other mental health professionals as fully qualified practitioners.

The site of practice has also shifted over the years—mainly to private offices and away from psychiatric hospitals and facilities. In the early 1950s, there was much hope for community mental health centers as places where outpatient services would replace the hospital for treating serious mental health problems. The removal of patients from facilities has occurred in most states, but the services offered in the community centers has fallen far short of the need. To add to the gulf in mental health services (between needs of patients and services of providers), most private practitioners preferred treating the "walking worried" or problems of living, which lends itself to briefer, more successful treatment. The latter two criteria are also favored by third-party payers, who have grown in presence and power over the years. It is arguable as to who will determine the psychotherapy of the future—therapists themselves or employees of health insurance companies.

The practice of psychotherapy has changed dramatically over the last 100 years. For a fuller view of these changes, see Freedheim (1992).

PROFESSIONAL TRAINING

The aims and curricula of professional training for psychologists have gone through a number of phases over the years, most notably during the time of the Colorado Conference in 1949, where the tone was set for training in clinical psychology. The "Boulder Model" has held sway in the field until most recently. It is no longer "in vogue" for clinical training programs to maintain the dual purpose of scientist-professional. Many programs give much greater emphasis to one or the other, with a growing number of professional schools focusing on clinical application rather than clinical research. The turn away from the principles enunciated at the Colorado Conference had its roots in an experimental PsyD (doctorate of psychology) program at the University of Illinois in 1968 (Peterson 1992). Although no longer in operation, it was the progenitor of over 20 such programs throughout the United States and is the fastest growing influence in graduate training in psychology. Last year (1991), over one-third of the doctoral degrees awarded in psychology were given by PsyD programs.

A LOOK TOWARD THE FUTURE

In reviewing the historical perspectives of psychotherapy, the author, with J. Norcross (Norcross and Freedheim 1992) distilled six emergent themes as having a bearing on our present thinking and most probably the immediate future of the field. These are pluralism, contextualism, prescriptionism, therapeutic alliance, economic pressures, and process-outcome linkages.

Pluralism

Not long ago in our history, psychotherapy was practiced almost exclusively in an individual format, in private offices, and with limited clientele. In today's practice, we see an ever-expanding host of settings, from clinics to community centers, and in specialized environments, such as prisons, schools, and even locker rooms (Feldman 1991). Our pluralism extends to increasingly diverse population groups, as well as to a much fuller range of intervention approaches and techniques.

In addition, whereas the field was initially dominated by psychiatrists and analysts, psychotherapy is now conducted primarily by nonmedical clinicians. Psychologists well outnumber psychiatrists, and social workers outnumber both of them combined.

Contextualism

Psychotherapy is no longer conducted in isolation. In addition to the client and the therapist, there is often a "third party" involved, with its own demands and agenda. We will have to accommodate to the new models of mental-health delivery, as there will be no alternatives (Austad and Hoyt 1992). In addition to therapy with some "over the shoulder" looks from outside, various treatment approaches are being carried out in contexts that would be entirely foreign and rejected a decade ago. For example, the contingencies in the environment that behavior therapists traditionally focus upon are expanding to broader social and community concerns (Glass and Arnkoff 1992). Likewise, psychoanalysis has reconceptualized change in the individual as more "context-dependent, a process subject to the situational, interpersonal, as well as intrapsychic influences" (Liff, 1992).

Researchers in psychotherapy are realizing that the meaning of therapists' as well as clients' behavior is best seen in a context and not in isolation from the environment (Heatherington 1989).

Prescriptionism

Psychotherapy has strenuously avoided prescriptive treatments, mainly because we have just not been able to develop any kind of coherent specificity of approach to specific ailments. Although it is a goal that still lies in the somewhat distant future, psychotherapists will eventually find treatments that do fit the problems. "Prescriptionism" means finding that particular match among client, disorder, and treatment (Norcross 1991). Hopefully, we will not require a unique therapist for each prescription, although all therapists know that there are problems and certain clients that just cannot be treated by any therapist. Adding this fourth element—the therapist—to the formula only further complicates the picture. We have come far in specialty treatments for many problems (e.g., addictions), but the development of treatment plans has far to go.

Therapeutic Alliance

If psychotherapy researchers and practitioners can agree on anything, it is the significance of developing a therapeutic relationship as a necessary component of the vast majority of treatment situations. In fact there is a strong consensus that therapeutic alliance is the one common factor in successful therapy that transcends all other factors (Grencavage and Norcross 1990). Behavior therapists and psychoanalysts appear to agree that the relationship in therapy is emerging as the strongest predictor of outcome (Eagle and Wolitzky 1992).

Economic Pressures

The emergence of the third party in therapy has been referred to above, and its presence is clearly driven by economic forces. The zooming cost of health care has not been concentrated in the area of mental health. Yet, the widespread need and growing use of mental health counselors has made our area a visible target for trimming costs in the health field (Adams 1992). Unfortunately, the extent and availability of psychotherapy may be determined more by economic concerns than by health needs in the future.

Process-Outcome Linkages

The current gap between process researchers and outcome evaluators appears to be diminishing with better understanding of each other and a growing appreciation that emphasis on one over the other is nonproductive (Beutler 1990). As the distinction between process and outcome research fades, the linkages between the two are being forged. Today, more researchers are finding that therapeutic outcomes may be due the transactions between clients and therapists.

Another aspect of the process-outcome paradigm might be seen in the area of training, in which studies of training components (process) must be linked with clinical competence.

Psychotherapy has travelled a complex, if not lengthy, journey. As the field continues to expand, the challenges to develop standards of excellence in training and practice become increasingly more difficult. Hopefully, the resolve and dedication of researchers in the field will not be diminished in the century ahead.

REFERENCES

ADAMS, D. B. 1992. The future roles of psychotherapy in the medical-surgical arena. Psychotherapy 29.
ARKOWITZ, H. 1992. Integrative theories of therapy. *In* History of Psychotherapy:

A Century of Change. D. K. Freedheim, Ed.: 261–303. American Psychological Association. Washington, D.C.

AUSTAD, C. S. & M. F. HOYT. 1992. The managed care movement and the future of psychotherapy. Psychotherapy. 29: 109–118.

AZRIN, N. H. 1977. A strategy for applied research: Learning based but outcome oriented. Am. Psychol. 30: 469–485.

BANDURA, A. 1982. Self-efficacy mechanisms in human agency. Am. Psychol. 37: 122–147.

BEUTLER, L. E. 1990. Introduction to the special series on advances in psychotherapy process research. J. Consult. Clin. Psychol. 58: 263–264.

BROTEMARKLE, R. A. 1947. Fifty years of clinical psychology: Clinical psychology 1896–1946. J. Consult. Psychol. 11: 1–4.

CATTELL, R. B. 1954. The meaning of clinical psychology. In An Introduction to Clinical Psychology, 2nd ed. L. A. Pennington & I. A. Berg, Eds.: 3–25. Ronald Press. New York.

CUSHMAN, P. 1992. Psychotherapy to 1992: A historically situated interpretation. In History of Psychotherapy: A Century of Change. D. K. Freedheim, Ed.: 21–64. American Psychological Association. Washington, D.C.

EAGLE, M. N. & D. L. WOLITZKY. 1992. Psychoanalytic theories of psychotherapy. In History of Psychotherapy: A Century of Change. D. K. Freedheim, Ed.: 109–158. American Psychological Association. Washington, D.C.

EYSENCK, H. J. 1952. The effects of psychotherapy: An evaluation. J. Consult. Psychol. 16: 319–324.

FELDMAN, L. 1991. Strikeouts and psycho-outs. The New York Times Magazine July 7: 10–13.

FENICHEL, O. 1930. Ten years of the Berlin Psychoanalytic Institute, 1920–1930. Berlin Psychoanalytic Institute. Berlin.

FISHMAN, D. B. & C. M. FRANKS. 1992. Evolution and differentiation within behavior therapy: A theoretical and epistemological review. In History of Psychotherapy: A Century of Change. D. K. Freedheim Ed.: 159–196. American Psychological Association. Washington, D.C.

FRANK, J. D. 1992. The Johns Hopkins Psychotherapy Research Project. In History of Psychotherapy: A Century of Change. D. K. Freedheim, Ed.: 392–396. American Psychological Association. Washington, D.C.

FREEDHEIM, D. K., Ed. 1992. History of Psychotherapy: A Century of Change. American Psychological Association. Washington, D.C.

GLASS, C. R. & D. B. ARNKOFF. 1992. Behavior therapy. In History of Psychotherapy: A Century of Change. D. K. Freedheim, Ed.: 587–628. American Psychological Association. Washington, D.C.

GRENCAVAGE, L. M. & J. C. NORCROSS. 1990. Where are the commonalities among the therapeutic common factors? Prof. Psychol. Res. Pract. 21: 372–378.

HEATHERINGTON, L. 1989. Toward more meaningful clinical research. Psychotherapy 26: 436–447.

LIFF, Z. A. 1992. Psychoanalysis and dynamic techniques. In History of Psychotherapy: A Century of Change. D. K. Freedheim, Ed.: 571–586. American Psychological Association. Washington, D.C.

NORCROSS, J. C. 1991. Prescriptive matching in psychotherapy. Psychotherapy 28: 439–443.

NORCROSS, J. C. & D. K. FREEDHEIM. 1992. Into the future: Retrospect and prospect in psychotherapy. In History of Psychotherapy: A Century of Change. D. K.

Freedheim, Ed.: 881–900. American Psychological Association. Washington, D.C.

PETERSON, D. R. 1992. The doctor of psychology degree. *In* History of Psychotherapy: A Century of Change. D. K. Freedheim, Ed.: 829–849. American Psychological Association. Washington, D.C.

RICE, L. N. & L. S. GREENBERG. 1992. Humanistic approaches to psychotherapy. *In* History of Psychotherapy: A Century of Change. D. K. Freedheim, Ed.: 197–224. American Psychological Association. Washington, D.C.

ROGERS, C. R. 1942. Counseling and Psychotherapy. Houghton Mifflin. Boston, MA.

SMITH, M. L., G. V. GLASS & T. I. MILLER. 1980. The Benefits of Psychotherapy. Johns Hopkins University Press. Baltimore, MD.

STRUPP, H. H. & K. I. HOWARD. 1992. A brief history of psychotherapy research. *In* History of Psychotherapy: A Century of Change. D. K. Freedheim, Ed.: 309–334. American Psychological Association. Washington, D.C.

WALLERSTEIN, R. S. 1986. Forty-two Lives in Treatment: A Study of Psychoanalysis and Psychotherapy. Guilford Press. New York.

WOLPE, J. 1958. Psychotherapy by Reciprocal Inhibition. Stanford University Press. Stanford, CA.

G. Stanley Hall and Company: Observations on the First 100 APA Presidents

JOHN D. HOGAN[a]

Department of Psychology
St. John's University
Jamaica, New York 11439

G. Stanley Hall referred to the American Psychological Association (APA) only once in his autobiography (Hall 1923), and that reference is brief and part of a list. Similarly, biographies of William James and George T. Ladd yield scant reference to the APA. It would be easy to conclude that these early leaders of psychology did not realize the importance of the organization they helped to shape. It is almost certain, moreover, that they would be astonished at the size and scope of their organization today.

With the presidential term of Charles D. Spielberger, the list of APA presidents reached 100. The number alone evokes a call for some kind of review of APA leaders, no matter how personally or professionally disparate and chronologically diverse they may be. Before proceeding, however, there are two points that require classification. First, it should be noted that Charles Spielberger was the 100th president, but not the last of 100 *different* presidents. Two presidents were each elected to two terms: G. Stanley Hall (1892 and 1924) and William James (1894 and 1904). Spielberger served the 100th presidential term, but 97 different individuals served terms before him. Second, and this has been a matter of some confusion, it should also be noted that the numbering of the presidents and the numbering of annual meetings do not correspond. (For example, Spielberger, the 100th president, presided over the 99th annual meeting.) In 1929, the 9th International Congress of Psychology met in New Haven, and the APA, in effect, cancelled its meeting in favor of the international one. Although arrangements were made for APA president Karl Lashley to deliver his presidential address before the Congress, the APA has never counted this meeting as one of its own.

[a]Address for correspondence: 222 Martling Avenue, Tarrytown, New York 10591.

Educational Background

Most APA presidents, not surprisingly, have earned a Ph.D. degree in psychology. However, a number of them had other degrees. William James, for instance, held an M.D. degree, and Hugo Münsterberg held both the Ph.D. and the M.D. (James did not have a high regard for the M.D. degree; Münsterberg recommended both degrees as the best combination for a psychologist.) George T. Ladd was, for a time, a practicing minister and had earned a Doctor of Divinity (D.D.) degree. It may be splitting hairs, but several APA presidents had Ph.D. degrees in philosophy. They included James M. Baldwin, John Dewey, Josiah Royce, and Edwin R. Guthrie. Of course, there were several presidents with no doctoral degree at all.

Mary Whiton Calkins, the first woman president of the APA (1905), had no doctoral degree, but it was not for lack of trying. She completed all the requirements, but was denied the degree by Harvard because she was a woman. APA president James Rowland Angell (1906) never returned to Germany to put his dissertation into more acceptable German and hence was not granted the degree. (In a related version of the story, Angell did not complete the degree because he chose to return to the United States to be married.) Henry R. Marshall (APA president 1907) did not have a permanent university affiliation and was a practicing architect all of his life. Presumably, the doctoral degree was not of great importance to him. George S. Fullerton (APA president 1896), who presided over the organizational meeting of the APA and taught at several institutions of higher learning, including the University of Pennsylvania, Columbia, University, the University of Vienna, and Vassar College, had as his terminal degree the M.A. The most curious case may be Howard C. Warren (APA president 1913). He studied at Leipzig but did not complete his degree. Several years after his APA presidential term, he was granted his doctorate "by special arrangement" with Johns Hopkins University.

Altogether, 94 individuals who served as APA president had doctoral degrees of one kind or another. However, their degrees were from only 27 different institutions. Eight schools account for 63 presidents, or 67% of the total. Those eight schools, and the number of presidents to whom they granted doctoral level degrees, were as follows: Columbia University, 14; Harvard University, 13; Cornell University, 7; Johns Hopkins University, 7; Yale University, 7; the University of Chicago, 6; the University of Leipzig, 5; and the University of Iowa, 4. In addition to Leipzig, the only other foreign universities to have granted the doctorate to APA presidents were the University of Berlin, 2, and the University of Halle, 1. The only West Coast universities contributing presidents were Stanford University, 3, and the University of California, Berkeley, 1.

Mentors

Several teachers became formal mentors to a number of students who would eventually become APA presidents. In fact, for a time it seemed the easiest path to the APA presidency was through the proper choice of a mentor. James McKeen Cattell holds the record for mentoring the most APA presidents. A former APA president himself (1895), he served as mentor to seven psychologists who later became APA presidents. They were Edward L. Thorndike (APA president 1912), Robert S. Woodworth (1914), Shepherd I. Franz (1920), Harry Hollingworth (1927), Albert Poffenberger (1935), John F. Dashiell (1938), and Herbert Woodrow (1941). Edward B. Titchener, although never an APA president, (the APA had trouble keeping him as a member!), served as mentor to six individuals who would later become APA presidents: Walter B. Pillsbury (APA president 1910), John W. Baird (1918), Margaret F. Washburn (1921), Madison Bentley (1925), Edwin G. Boring (1928), and J. P. Guilford (1950). Other mentors with more than one student who became an APA president include James Rowland Angell with five, G. Stanley Hall with four, and Hugo Münsterberg with four. Of course, Cattell, Titchener, and Münsterberg each had Wilhelm Wundt as their formal mentor, making Wundt the "super-mentor."

The intergenerational passing of the APA presidential mantle is not uncommon. Many presidents have had other presidents in their intellectual ancestry. In this regard, none has so distinguished a genealogy as Anne Anastasi (APA president 1972). Her mentor of record was Henry E. Garrett (APA president 1946), whose mentor was Robert S. Woodworth (APA president 1914), who in turn was mentored by James McKeen Cattell (APA president 1895).

Age

As a group, the earliest APA presidents were young, although the average age of presidents has increased with each succeeding decade. The median age of the first ten presidents was 38, a surprisingly low figure in view of the relatively advanced age of the first three presidents. G. Stanley Hall was 48 during his first term, George T. Ladd was 51, and William James was 52. Then again, Hugo Münsterberg, the seventh APA president, was 34 when elected and 35 during half his term. James McKeen Cattell, the fourth APA president, was also 34 when elected, but is second in presidential youth. During Cattell's presidential year, he was a week older than Münsterberg would be during his term.

Other APA presidents serving terms while still in their thirties include George S. Fullerton, James M. Baldwin, Joseph Jastrow, John B. Watson, Walter Pillsbury, and Karl Lashley. There have been none as young since Lashley in 1929, although several presidents have been in their early forties. The only presidents to begin terms in their 70s were Wolfgang Köhler (1959) and G. Stanley Hall (1924). Hall was the oldest elected president at age 79 (his second term), but he died before the year was out, the only APA president to die in office. In the last decade, the median age for APA presidents was 62. The median (and modal) age of the first 100 presidents, in their presidential year, was 50 years.

While on the subject of age, there is some evidence that APA presidents tend to live longer than the average. The median lifespan of the first 50 presidents, now all deceased, was 75 years. (In 1900, the projected lifespan in the United States was 46 years. The median year of birth for this group was 1873.) Furthermore, the first 50 presidents were not required to be long-lived in order to be rewarded with the APA presidency. Their median age in their presidential year was only 46. On average, they lived almost 30 years beyond their year of office.

Seven of the first 50 presidents lived into their 90s, including John Dewey, 92, and Walter R. Miles, 93. William L. Bryan died at age 95, the longest-lived APA president so far. On the other hand, John W. Baird died only a few months after his year of office and was, at age 49, the shortest-lived APA president.

Gender

Women have not been represented among APA presidents in proportion to their number in the organization; there have been only seven women presidents in 100 years. Mary Whiton Calkins was the first woman APA president and, at age 42, the youngest woman president. She was also the only woman represented at the first APA Meeting in December 1892. (E. C. Sanford read research reports based on the work of several of his students, including a report by Calkins on "Statistics of Dreams.") Calkins was the only woman present at the second APA meeting in 1893, the year she was elected to APA membership and, by her presence, became the first woman to attend an APA meeting. (Christine Ladd-Franklin was also elected to APA membership in 1893, but did not attend the annual meeting.)

After the election of Margaret Floy Washburn as the second woman APA president in 1921, it would be 51 years before another woman served in that high office. Then, two women were elected consecutively, Anne Anastasi (1972) and Leona Tyler (1973). Anastasi, by the way, was the APA president to receive the doctoral degree at the youngest age—she was 21 at the time. However, Münsterberg and Köhler were only slightly older. The typical APA president received the doctorate at the advanced age of 26!

Points of Origin

Most APA presidents were born in the continental United States, but 11 were not. George S. Fullerton was born in Fatehgarh, India, and Charles H. Judd was born in Bareilly, India. Five presidents were born in Europe: Hugo Münsterberg (Danzig, East Prussia), Joseph Jastrow (Warsaw, Poland), Carl Seashore (Morlunda, Sweden), Wolfgang Köhler (Reval, Estonia), and Joseph Matarazzo (Caiazzo, Italy). Three others were born in Canada: John W. Baird (Motherwell, Ontario), Donald Hebb (Chester, Nova Scotia), and Albert Bandura (Mundare, Alberta). Kenneth B. Clark, the only Black psychologist to serve as APA president (1971), was born in the Panama Canal Zone.

Of the APA presidents born in the United States, the greatest number were from New York, with eleven presidents, and Pennsylvania with ten. Eight of those from New York State were born in New York City; five of those from Pennsylvania were born in Philadelphia. Other well-represented states are California with seven presidents, and Massachusetts and Indiana with six each. Overall, small towns were more likely to be the birthplace when compared to large towns and cities. These small towns include such exotic locales as Grass Valley, California (Josiah Royce); Belchertown, Massachusetts (Robert Woodworth); Two Harbors, Minnesota (Donald Marquis); Greenland Gap, West Virginia (Quinn McNemar); and Jasper, Alabama (Ray Fowler).

Parents of APA presidents were apparently fond of traditional first names, despite the occurrence of the occasional Granville (G. Stanley Hall), Orval (O. H. Mowrer), or Joy (J. P. Guilford). Six presidents were named John, five were named George, and four each were named Joseph, Robert, or Walter. Middle names are a little less conventional, and include such entries as Broadus (John B. Watson), Ivory (Shepherd I. Franz), Garrigues (Edwin G. Boring), Chace (Edward C. Tolman), Ransom (Carl R. Rogers), and Ropiequet (Ernest R. Hilgard).

For unknown reasons, January was the most popular month of birth for APA presidents, with 14. November is next, with 12 presidents. May and June each have 11. Only two presidents were born in September.

A Composite Portrait

All these data suggest a modal APA president for the first 100 years: a 50-year-old male, with a doctoral degree from Columbia or Harvard University, who was born in January in New York City, and whose first name was John. Not surprisingly, no APA president with that precise description existed in this cohort. There is one president, however, who comes close to fitting that description: William James—a 52-year-old male, with an M.D. degree from Harvard, who was born January 11, 1842, in the Astor House, down near New York's City Hall. All things considered, not a bad standard for the first 100 years. Not a bad standard at all.

REFERENCES

AMERICAN PSYCHOLOGICAL ASSOCIATION. 1989. Directory of the American Psychological Association 1989. American Psychological Association. Washington, DC.

FERNBERGER, S. W. 1932. The American Psychological Association: A historical summary, 1892–1930. Psychol. Bull. 29(1): 1–89.

HALL, G. S. 1923. Life and Confessions of a Psychologist. D. Appleton. New York.

HILGARD, E. R., Ed. 1978. American Psychology in Historical Perspective: Addresses of the Presidents of the American Psychological Association, 1892–1977. American Psychological Association. Washington, D.C.

HILGARD, E. R. 1987. Psychology in America: A Historical Survey. Harcourt Brace Jovanovich. New York.

HOGAN, J. D. & V. S. SEXTON. 1992. Women and the American Psychological Association. Psychol. of Women Quart 15: 623–634.

MISIAK, H. & V. S. SEXTON. 1966. History of Psychology: An Overview. Grune & Stratton. New York.

SOKAL, M. M. 1973. APA's first publication: Proceedings of the American Psychological Association, 1892–1893. Am. Psychol. 28: 277–292.

ZUSNE, L. 1975. Names in the History of Psychology: A Biographical Sourcebook. Hemisphere. Washington, DC.

Sitzfleisch 2: The Platzgeist and Cognitive Environmental Psychology

KURT SALZINGER

Department of Psychology
Hofstra University
Hempstead, New York 11550

There is a special purgatory reserved here on Earth for those of us who comply with an order to act as discussants. We are required to discuss papers that we never see beforehand, that are often presented by people we did not expect, who speak in a tone and form just barely understandable to us because we are sitting on the dais, where it is difficult to hear the speaker, and then we have to comment on slides presented in such a way that they are not visible or at least greatly distorted from the discussant's vantage point.

Now this is not my first sentence as discussant, and as a result I have learned to cope after a fashion. The first thing I've learned to do is to ignore completely the papers I am expected to comment on. I sometimes look busy writing while the speakers talk in order to worry them at least a little bit with the suspicion that I will indulge in a scathing attack on whatever they have to say, when in fact, I am preparing my own totally unrelated paper.

With that introduction, let me go directly to my own paper. This is a follow-up of an essay that I presented some years ago, and has been included in a book edited by Bob Rieber and myself (Salzinger 1980). Its title was a little long, but because of that it served to summarize the paper's contents. The title was: "Sitzfleisch, the Zeitgeist, and the Hindsightgeist." If I had been permitted to give a paper instead of being banished to the discussant slot, I would have called it: Sitzfleisch 2: The Platzgeist and Cognitive Environmental Psychology.[a] You will no doubt ask after reading my paper— that is, if you are still reading—what has this got to do with "cognitive"? My answer is that I have become aware in the last few years that the adjective "cognitive" is obligatory for any paper in psychology. It is to be attached to any mention of psychology these days if one is to have an audience for one's papers. I am using the word "cognitive" simply as an attention-getting device. In addition, just because I'm a behavior analyst I do not want you to think that I do not think, if you know what I mean.

But enough of this procrastination. Although everybody will have something to say about the power of the *Zeitgeist,* I wish to point to the power of the *Platzgeist,* the spirit of the place. We are here celebrating two anniversaries: the 100th anniversary of the American Psychological Association and

---

[a]As you can see from the title, the editors relented.

the 175th anniversary of the New York Academy of Sciences. Since they obviously do not have in common the same *Zeitgeist,* we must resort to the corresponding concept, that of the *Platzgeist,* keeping in mind a large *Platz,* a large environment, namely the United States.

All of which leads me back to my earlier paper, which, as at least some of you recall, dealt with Dr. Urpsyche, the German psychologist who immigrated to the United States and was active here around the time of the signing of the Declaration of Independence. After he published his book called *Mach Schnell—Do it Quickly*—(it was published in German in the United States only and thus never did get the audience it deserved), he was made an Honorary Fellow of the Society of Schnell Machen, an organization which preceded both the APA and the Academy. Later, he was elected President when he had almost finished his second book, *Mach Schneller (Do it Faster).* Both books were devoted, as you might have guessed, to reaction time. Dr. Urpsyche's students, who were less serious than their mentor, called themselves the Schnell Macher's League. Eventually, Dr. Urpsyche lost interest in reaction time—indeed he eventually thought that the essence of psychology lay in responding as slowly as you can—and wrote his anti-reaction time tome, called *Mach es schon Langsam (Do it slowly)* and was read out of the very organization he had helped to organize and over which he had presided as president.

When I last reported on Dr. Urpsyche, I was just beginning to go through the many papers that I had fortuitously come upon. As you no doubt recall, somebody had left them in a large six-foot stack blocking my way into my apartment. Anyway, I have ever since been working my way through that stack and recently came upon mention of a descendant who also became a psychologist. Her name was Wilhelmina, clearly named after our hero of yesteryear, Wilhelm Urpsyche. Wilhelmina Urpsyche, born in 1836, so identified with her great-granduncle that she also published all her work in German, and also in the United States. One is tempted to seek out a gene for perishing on account of publishing in the wrong places, but that discussion will have to await another paper. Here, I am just trying to explain why her name is not any better known to this audience than is her ancestor's. In any case, her work took off from Wilhelm's idea of responding slowly.

"What," she said, "would have been the reason for my uncle's resorting to this *Mach Langsam* approach to psychology?" Brilliant as she was, she finally figured it out. What people do, while responding slowly, is think. And thus was cognitive psychology born. She wrote her most significant book, whose title she translated as *I Am Slow, Therefore I Think* at the very beginning of her very busy career. It seems to me that with this book she started the tradition of the slow-thinking cognitive psychologists of today. The pages of her book that came into my possession were filled with diagrams that we would call flow charts today. Here is an example of one:

Ich bemuehe mich langsam zu arbeiten → Ich arbeite langsam → Deswegen denke ich → Deswegen denke ich: Warum arbeite ich so langsam? → Ich hoere auf langsam zu arbeiten → Ich hoere auf zu denken → Gott sei Dank!

I try to work slowly → I work slowly → Therefore, I think → Therefore, I think: Why do I work so slowly? → I stop working slowly → I stop thinking → Thank God!

Towards the end of her career she was working so slowly and thinking so often that she was finally killed by a horse and carriage that was just sauntering along; neither the driver nor the horse believed that she would not get out of the way in time. It was a tragic loss for psychology because she was just about to produce a real breakthrough in what we now call cognitive psychology—at least that is what her notes kept saying. She wrote (and I quote), "Ich denke und denke and denke, und so weiter." She came to call it her "und so weiter" theory. In translation, this means, "I think and think and think, and so on." The theory was called the "and so on" theory. I cannot say that I fully understand this theory except that it has a very contemporary ring about it.

There are some other interesting tidbits about her that I would like to share with you. Among them are the ways she used to inspire her students. One of the terms she used quite often has come down to us in the form of a frequently seen advertisement. I am sure you've all seen or heard of the Volkswagen ad about *Fahrvergnuegen*. Well, I cannot tell you how an American advertising firm got hold of Wilhelmina's work, but I think it is beyond the realm of belief to suggest that they were not influenced by Wilhelmina's original idea. Clearly, she had had nothing to say about cars—there were none when she coined her own use of the word *Vergnuegen*—although she might well have had something to say about horses and carriages. Anyhow, in an attempt to get her students interested in research, she used to speak of *Forschvergnuegen* to them. *Forschvergnuegen,* as everybody knows, means "research pleasure," something we all should be telling our students about.

Wilhelmina Urpsyche used to give a *Forschvergnuegen* award to the student who best approximated that Holy Grail of Slow Responding in her or his experiment of slow-time reaction time. Competition got to be so fierce, with students trying to get the slowest reaction time possible, that some subjects almost starved to death before the experimental procedure allowed them to respond to the stimulus. As you might imagine, such slow reactions resulted in slow publication, with the consequence that people like James McKeen Cattell, the first psychologist to have headed the New York Academy of Sciences and an expert in reaction time, were entirely ignorant of slow cognitive psychology and, of course, of Dr. Wilhelmina Urpsyche. And so ends the sad story of one of our most interesting ancestors in psychology—a psychologist who did her work very much alone in her time (independent of the *Zeitgeist*) and apparently very much independent of her place (independent of the *Platzgeist*). Important as the *Platzgeist* is with respect to other psychologists, it failed to affect her work because of the strange interaction of its theoretical structure and the practical needs of the publication market place. I will leave to another time discussion of the effect of publication opportunities and the *Platzgeist* or perhaps one of you will wish to study that seminal concept.

REFERENCE

SALZINGER, K. 1980. Sitzfleisch, the Zeitgeist, and the Hindsightgeist. *In* Psychology: Theoretical-Historical Perspectives. R. Rieber & K. Salzinger, Eds. Academic Press. New York.

Subject Index

Index of Contributors